The Geography of God's Mercy

To my brothers and sisters and their spouses,

with love and gratitude.

The Geography of God's Mercy
Stories of Compassion and Forgiveness

Patrick Hannon, CSC

THE GEOGRAPHY OF GOD'S MERCY
Stories of Compassion and Forgiveness
by Patrick Hannon, CSC

Edited by Gregory F. Augustine Pierce
Cover design by Tom A. Wright
Cover art by Martin Nguyen
Text design and typesetting by Patricia A. Lynch

"In the Dark" was first published as "Depressed, Who Me?" In *Hidden Presence: Twelve Blessings That Transformed Sorrow and Loss* (ACTA Publications, 2003).

Scripture quotations are from the *Newly Revised Standard Version Bible*, copyright © 1989 by the Division of Christian Education of the National Council of the Churches of Christ in the USA. Used by permission.

Published by ACTA Publications, 5559 W. Howard Street, Skokie, IL 60077-2621, (800) 397-2282, www.actapublications.com

Library of Congress Catalog number: 2007927591

Hardcover ISBN: 978-0-87946-332-8
Softcover ISBN: 978-0-87946-333-5

Printed in Canada by Graphics244

Year 15 14 13 12 11 10 09 08 07
Printing 15 14 13 12 11 10 9 8 7 6 5 4 3 2 First

Text is printed on 100% post-consumer waste recycled paper.

CONTENTS

I'll Keep You All for Another Day

I love the smell of Cream of Wheat. This bowl of mush has become for me what Kraft never intended it to be: a moment when I brush up against the memory of Monica Jane Lighthouse Hannon, aka Mom, leaning against the grizzled stove at dawn, her one hand holding a wooden spoon as she dutifully stirs the pot of porridge, while the other one dutifully holds, between its fingers, her Kool menthol cigarette half consumed. Her eyes are closed, and her dark-framed glasses are fogged over by the steam and she doesn't even know it. Takes a lickin' and keeps on tickin'. She was one tough lady, my mom.

The day before, Mike, Greg and I, all of us under the age of ten, were engaged in one of our epic battles over God-knows-what and were in the process of destroying our bedroom. At one point Greg pushed me against the wobbly bookcase, thus dispatching the Mason jar that held my toothpicked potato plant from the top shelf. It crashed to the ground, shattering into shards of glass. We knew there would be hell to pay because we could hear our mother already bounding down the stairs prepared to mete out the justice we knew would be ours. I, of course, instinctively made a beeline to the closet, believing religiously that its darkness would somehow swallow me up and make me disappear. En route my right foot stepped on one of the shards of glass, sending a shot of pain up my spine and into my brain and back again, an agonizing round trip.

There's my mother sitting next to me on the rumpus room stairs trying to dislodge the three-inch long piece of glass from my foot, pressing gently against the skin while ever-so-gingerly removing the glass splinter. Pressing a tad too hard, a loop of blood shoots out and hits her on the forehead, and she about faints. But my life is in her hands now, and she knows it and recovers. She rings Dad's secretary, who has to come and pick us up because it's Brian's sixteenth birthday and Dad and he have taken the station wagon to the Department of Motor Vehicles so Brian can take his driver's test.

There's my mother holding my hand in the operating room at Eden Hospital as the doctor stitches my wounded sole back together again. "Let's say some Hail Mary's," she says, and we rattle them off like nuns. "You're a brave boy," she whispers to me, her lips to my ear as I stifle my cries, and I almost believe her.

There's my mother running down the steep decline of Arcadian Drive, her fluffy slippers flopping away, chasing my brothers as they push me in the Romley's Market shopping cart later that afternoon, its rickety wheels *begging* for a rock big enough or a hole deep enough to send me and my tender foot catapulting into the thin air.

There's my mother leaning against the stove the next morning, like she is every single morning, stirring the Cream of Wheat, adding a dollop of butter and a generous sprinkling of brown sugar and, on good days, a touch of cinnamon.

And there she is ladling the creamy breakfast potage into bowls as her brood lumbers to the breakfast table with tangled hair, broken bones, blackened eyes, and wounded bodies stitched back together.

It was as if every morning Mom renewed her contract with us. Often she said it in so many words: All right, I'll keep you all for another day.

On bad days, when Mom was taking it from every direction, one of us (the youngest of us available at the time was usually drafted) would be sent to our mother after the dust had settled to ask her a simple question: "Mom, if you had to do it all over again, would you still have all of us kids?" She would sit there in a daze, mumbling incoherently, but we knew her answer would come loud and clear the next morning, when she made breakfast for us.

✦ ✦ ✦ ✦ ✦ ✦ ✦

When Mike was ten, he threw a hoe over the fence at Greg, who was nine, because Greg wouldn't let him pass through the tall wooden gate to the backyard. The sharp metal end of the hoe hit Greg on the crown of his head and they were both sent to bed that afternoon by Mrs. Trimble our babysitter, who never really knew what to do with juvenile delinquents *but* send them to bed. It didn't matter that Greg was bleeding like a stuck pig. To bed they went. You can only imagine what they looked like when Mom got home, something out of Truman Capote's *In Cold Blood*, no doubt. Years later, reflecting on that day, Mike remembers sitting with Mom at the kitchen table. "She looked at me with tears in her eyes and said, 'Michael, it's because of you I'm going to hell.'" The next morning, however, the slate was wiped clean, the contract renewed for another day, and we knew this, of course, because of the waft of Cream of Wheat that greeted us as we woke from slumber.

❀ ❀ ❀ ❀ ❀ ❀ ❀

These days, when it seems as if the weight of the world's sin is bearing down on me or when the burden of the sin of my own making leaves me gasping a bit, I make myself a bowl of Cream of Wheat. It doesn't so much take me back to the more innocent days of my youth—because, quite frankly, I wasn't so innocent then and neither was the world. But it does remind me that if my mother could be so forgiving of her brood, whose daily duty was to put one more gray hair in her scalp, how much more God forgives us for all our bone-headed, faith-defying, senseless and stupefying sins. Flannery O'Conner, the Catholic writer who grew up in what she referred to as "the Christ-haunted South," put it this way: "The world has, for all its horror, been found by God to be worth dying for." To this day I find that truth almost too much to bear.

Divine mercy—in the face of human selfishness and self-inflicted brokenness—is, to borrow a phrase from the explorer David Folsom, "a terrible beauty." Such an extravagant love stuns me by its power to heal, but it also scares me because in its healing wake it leaves me, at least for a while, disoriented. Is it really possible that mercy has lasting merit? Is it possible that the Cross of Christ really did save the whole world from the power of darkness? Can the last word really be love?

In a world humanly predicated on power and control, God's mercy draws its eternal strength from sacrifice. In a world where human justice is almost always laced with righteous vengeance, God's mercy strikes a discordant chord, at least when it hits the human ear, because it tells quite a different story: You are always welcomed back; you can always come back home. No life will ever be defined—at least by God—by its worst mistake or greatest sin.

❁ ❁ ❁ ❁ ❁ ❁

One evening Dad came home from work in a surly mood. He plopped himself down into his worn and weathered easy chair, snapped the evening paper open in one motion, took a long sip from his hastily concocted bourbon and water, and dared anyone to disturb him. Most of us wisely retreated to quiet corners of the house, but not Brian and Jack. They were arguing—oblivious to the wisp of steam rising from the awaking volcano nearby—in their bedroom located off the living room. They were fighting over whose turn it was to use the state-of-the-art manual typewriter Mom had picked up for them earlier that day, as a surprise, from the business supply rental store in town. She had rented it for the week to the tune of twenty bucks.

No life will ever be defined

—at least by God—

by its worst mistake

or greatest sin.

When the argument reached its fever pitch and they were tugging on the typewriter, each brother refusing to surrender, Dad appeared before them. "I'll solve this problem for you," he said as he took the typewriter from their grimy hands. As he raised the typewriter over his head in preparation for dropping it definitively to the ground, Mom appeared in the near distance. As Dad released his hands, we could all hear her scream, "Don't, Bill! It's a rental!" The word *rental* lingered there in the air as the typewriter made its way inexorably to the bedroom floor, shattering into a hundred pieces. Dad returned to his paper and evening cocktail without saying a word. All of us assembled in Brian and Jack's bedroom and, along with our mother, dropped to our knees and scooped up all the pieces of typewriter we could find. And for the next hour we tried to put that typewriter back together, in utter silence, lest we stir the volcanic giant again.

As it turned out, we tossed the machine away. But it was the face of our mother as she watched us unceremoniously deposit the typewriter in the garbage can that stays with me to this day. You could tell she was replaying the whole episode in her mind and actually enjoying it, for the faintest hint of a smile appeared on her face, one that said clearly to me, "Ah, now this is a story we'll be telling for a long, long time." And she was right.

The sin of that day surrendered to the story that has over the years fed the Hannon clan with side-aching laughter. I remember something Thomas Merton once wrote about sin that reflects perfectly that day years ago: "Even sin has played an unwilling part in saving sinners, for the infinite mercy of God cannot be prevented from drawing the greatest good out of the greatest evil." It is a fitting punishment to sin: to so bathe it in the waters of merciful laughter that eventually it no longer looks like itself anymore.

❁ ❁ ❁ ❁ ❁ ❁ ❁

God's mercy permeates all things. It is the air we breathe, the water we drink, and the bread we eat; and with each passing day I become more aware of the truth that God's glory shines most brightly through mercy, that God's power and might finds its greatest strength in compassion and forgiveness. For when God's mercy takes hold of us, the human heart comes to believe once again that broken bones, broken spirits, broken lives, and even broken typewriters will never have the last word. Like soothing waters, mercy washes over us and removes the stain of guilt and shame and dares us to imagine a life untangled from the snare of sin. I can't imagine anything bringing more glory to God than that. More than any other song, it is the song of mercy that resounds through all of creation.

"Let the heavens be glad, and let the earth rejoice," the psalmist sings in Psalm 96. "Let the sea roar and all that fills it; let the field exalt and everything in it. Then shall all the trees of the forest sing for joy before the LORD; for he is coming." Later, Isaiah 42 would add coastlands and deserts and mountaintops to this cacophony of nature.

The stories of this book echo this hymn to the geography of God's mercy. The earth, our home and God's home, sings of the glory of God and its melody is mercy. It is a terrible beauty, this song of God's love, because it draws us ever more deeply, if we let it, into the mysterious power that forgives and heals and makes whole, all the while stripping away all that protects us and holds us back. In the end, we come to surrender to this song's refrain, words of hope tripping from the very lips of God, a promise sealed with a merciful kiss: "All right," God sings, in so many words, "I'll keep you all for another day." And we know that He really means forever.

✿ ✿ ✿ ✿ ✿ ✿ ✿

Patrick Hannon, CSC
Colorado Springs, Colorado
Good Friday, 2007

ONE

A Dwelling in the Forest
The Silent Work of Mercy

Do not fear, O Jacob my servant,
Jeshuron whom I have chosen.
For I will pour water on the thirsty land,
and streams on the dry ground;
I will pour my spirit upon your descendents,
and my blessing on your offspring.
They shall spring up like a green tamarisk,
like willows by flowing streams.

Isaiah 44

The Trees that Transcend Fear

Apparently when you grow old, sometimes all you have left to show for your life is a squeaky electronic appliance of a piano. And a bed with a threadbare quilt neatly pressed upon it by the window. And a chair that faces a wall of framed photographed faces frozen in time smiling back at you. Such a fate it is for some, Shakespeare's sixth age on life's stage, when the clothes hang generously upon the bony frame and the stentorian voice "turns again towards childish treble" and the sturdy oak of one's dreams is whittled down seemingly.

And then, there's Catherine.

I visit Catherine on the first Friday of every other month. She's eighty-two years old now and lives by herself in a small room in an assisted care facility in Colorado Springs. Hers are the rasping piano and quilted bed by the window and chair facing the wall of photographs. Her husband has gone to God and so has one of her daughters. She told me once that a well-meaning friend stopped by one day and gently upbraided her for her wall of smiling faces. "Why do you want to be reminded of all these people? It will only make you sad," the friend had said. "Of course they make me sad," Catherine explained to me, "but she didn't seem to understand that they also make me smile."

And why wouldn't they? They are photographs of husband and children and grandchildren, of kin and friends through the years. And she has a story that goes with each one. Over her bed there's a picture of her with her mom and dad, and she's just a wee child in a lace dress and shiny shoes. She hasn't told me the story that goes with that one yet.

❀ ❀ ❀ ❀ ❀ ❀ ❀

For barely a fortnight, the aspen of Colorado's high country are in full and glorious splendor. "Trembling poplars" they are called. They are the tree of the autumn equinox and of old age, and it's not hard to see why, if you know anything about the Rocky Mountain aspen: While individual aspens are relatively short-lived—about the span of a generous human life of eighty to a hundred years, a stand (or grove) of aspen, by virtue of its unique way of reproducing by root sprouts and not seedlings, can be over 8,000 years old. One aspen male clone in the Wasatch Mountains of Utah occupies over seventeen acres, has more than 47,000 stems (each "stem" is a separate aspen tree), and is said to be over one million years old. An ancient grove that springs eternal.

In the autumn cool the aspen's leaves are transformed and become, as it were, a deciduous acclamation of that particular life that springs from death, a lilting hymn of praise to the Creator who must, like all of us, quiver with joy every year when the aspen are ripe and turn to gold. They remind us that death never has the last word, that from the wood of the cross (carved from aspen wood no doubt) sprout blossoms still. As the story goes, in ancient Ireland the coffin maker's measuring rod, the stick he used to measure the corpse for the box, was fashioned from aspen wood, apparently to remind the dead that this was not the end.

It is the stillness of the aspen grove in autumn that entices us once again to consider the power of God, which is abiding and abundant, enduring and endless, and ultimately mysterious.

It is the stillness of the aspen grove in autumn that entices us once again to consider the power of God, which is abiding and abundant, enduring and endless, and ultimately mysterious. Each dangling golden leaf tangoing with the wind seems to testify to divine mercy's singular victory. Imagine then the forest of whispering aspen at dusk and hear with hope God's response to a weary world.

Resilient, abundant, prodigious, defiant, utterly majestic. And in the gloaming season, aspen are the most eloquent trees that transcend fear and, in a golden sweep of hope, hint of resurrection.

✤ ✤ ✤ ✤ ✤ ✤ ✤

Catherine has, in the autumn of her life, grown accustomed to the laughter that mingles naturally with her tears. She spends a lot of time these days quietly looking at the faces on her wall and remembering the stories that go with each of them. They are not unlike the golden leaves of the autumn aspen, those faces and their stories that evoke sweet sadness. The rustling golden leaves, like Catherine's photographs, echo on the wings of silence the voice of Yahweh spoken centuries ago to a people who once grew faint with fear. Like poplars beside the flowing waters, my darling Catherine, your descendants will spring up and flourish. You will endure. And so, there's no reason to be afraid anymore. The golden forest of autumn aspen tells us so.

She Didn't Have to Say a Word

J oyce Vanderpoorten sat three seats in front of me in the second grade, and on a day that surely snuck up on both of us, our paths crossed. It was at the perilous intersection of my unthinking cruelty and her unguarded gloom that we met. Such is the mercy of God that encounters like the one I had with Joyce can, with His meddling, change the course of a life. God knows it changed mine.

It was right before lunchtime. Sister Anna Maria, our teacher, instructed the girls to go first to retrieve their lunch bags from the back of the room. This was done in a very orderly fashion—as was expected by our beloved teacher—with the girls in the front proceeding first, then those sitting behind them going second, and so forth. Well, when Joyce made her way past my desk, I stuck my right leg out into the aisle. Joyce, as I remember, wasn't having a particularly good day; in fact, it seemed as if she rarely did. I seldom saw her smile. Maybe it was because she was such a tiny creature and a member of a large family, two predicaments we both shared. The runt of any litter, human or otherwise, is never expected to survive and thus is never taken seriously. Maybe it was because of this that Joyce seemed to nurture such a saturnine countenance, one that said in so many words, "Get out of my way or I'll pop you in the head." As a rule, I steered clear of Joyce on her bad days.

She was making a beeline to the back of the room that day, a diesel train run off its tracks, oblivious to anything or anyone in her path, including my leg purposefully sticking out. I remember Joyce sailing through the air before landing on her stomach. When she landed, her body bounced and then skidded to a stop. She was up and standing before anyone had the chance to giggle or gasp, and with the look she gave the entire room, only the most foolish among us would have dared laugh. She scanned every face for the slightest sign of guilt, and when her eyes met mine I thought for sure she had nailed me. Apparently my face betrayed nothing, and she moved on.

It was then, when I knew I was not going to get caught, that I first began to ponder life and its verities with a somber conscience. Up until that day, I honestly don't think I had ever gotten away with anything anyway. My mother was too smart, my father too savvy, and my brothers and sisters, all of them double agents, only too happy to play the informant. My brothers and sisters and I finked on each other for the sheer sport of it. Before I outgrew this tendency years later, it was worth the fist to the chops I would most assuredly receive later to see an older brother go down. But this was different. I know Joyce and I had never exchanged vows, but given our relatively low status along the food chain, it *felt* like she was bone of my bone and flesh of my flesh. Seeing her exposed and painfully vulnerable, wounded and ripe for the purposeful jibe and giggle, I knew I had betrayed her in some way. It didn't sit well in my seven-year-old gut.

So there I was after lunch on the playground, a seven-year-old existentialist, confronted with the awesome power of my freedom. I was terrified by it. I was introduced right then and there to the reality of the slippery slope. I could, with each choice I made, construct a life worthy of the man from Galilee, a statue of whom stared back at me every Sunday at church, or I could try to get away with everything, live a life on the lam until, eventually, the law would catch up and I would be thrown into the slammer. The choice was mine.

Johnny Cash recorded his hit "Folsom Prison Blues" around that time. Every so often, when my mood darkened, I would retrieve the album from my father's stack of records, slip the scratchy vinyl out of its sleeve, and listen to it on the console in the living room when no one else was around, just so I would never forget what happens to those who don't listen to their mothers and commit themselves to a life of crime. I found the tune catchy and its lyrics instructive:

> When I was just a baby, my mama told me, "Son,
> Always be a good boy; don't ever play with guns."
> But I shot a man in Reno, just to watch him die.
> When I hear that whistle blowin' I hang my head and cry.

"But if the wicked, turning from the wickedness they have committed, do what is right and just," the prophet Ezekiel preached, "they shall preserve their life; since they have turned away from all the sins they have committed, they shall surely live. They shall not die." On the playground that day I tried to work out in my own mind and make sense of the claim mercy had on me, which until that time had remained unarticulated. I had not yet developed the necessary vocabulary. Sister Anna Maria had not yet introduced me to the sacramental concepts of confession, penance, absolution, and how they all worked together to bring us into the presence of our merciful God who, thankfully, has a terrible memory when it comes to the sins that weigh down the penitent heart. With Joyce in my sights, I was flying solo.

I knew instinctively that God would forgive me this wicked sin, that somewhere on that slippery slope I would find sufficient traction from his grace to keep me from sliding into Folsom Prison. But how would I know when mercy had done its work? How would I know I was forgiven? There was the rub. For advice, I turned to the only one who could make everything right again, the one who could help me stay on the straight and narrow, the one who could help me retrieve

How would I know

when mercy had done its work?

How would I know

I was forgiven?

my dignity and virtue from the cold, sweaty hands of the devil. Later that afternoon, I spilled my guts to sixteen-year-old Margie Hight, my secret girlfriend, who lived across the street from me and was the woman I would marry in time if she would have me. She told me if I wished to avoid prison I needed to fess up and apologize to Joyce. So I did.

The next morning I stopped at Joyce's desk after sharpening my pencil for the fifteenth time, and with the softest voice I could muster, I told her I had tripped her yesterday and that I was sorry. I closed my eyes and braced myself for the punch in the face. None came. I opened my eyes and saw Joyce not even looking up. Had she even heard me?

"Joyce," I said a little bit louder, "did you...."

"I heard you," she said. Her eyes stared straight ahead; she betrayed no emotion one way or the other. Then she looked up at me with those dark penetrating eyes. As I made my way to my desk, I got the distinct impression that she would deal with me later.

At recess, Joyce hunted me down and cornered me behind the school incinerator and clobbered me over the head with her book bag; but I didn't mind. I deserved it, after all, and she did have the decency to dole out the punishment in private. It had become apparent to me anyway that Joyce was really the only one who could set me free from my guilt. If a lump on the head was the price for my freedom, so be it. Smarting from my injury, I retired to a secluded corner of the playground. No one could see me except for the occasional eighth grader sneaking back from Al's Food Market by way of the hole in the fence near me, but they could not have cared less.

Ten minutes later, however, Joyce appeared. I thought she had come to finish me off, so I steeled myself for battle. She reached into her red corduroy lunch bag to retrieve the revolver, but imagine my surprise when instead of a six-shooter, she held in her hand a Hostess Twinkie. She broke it in two and handed me a piece. I took it and I ate it.

There we were, two second graders, our soft underbellies exposed, our weakness shining for the whole world to see and scoff at, our little bodies hanging from our respective crosses. Humbled beyond measure by this unexpected kindness, I learned something about God's mercy I had never read in a book. The truth baffles me to this day, but I still believe it.

Apparently, God has a deep fondness toward the struggling sinner who is trying to mend his ways. Looking back on that day when Joyce shared half of her lunchtime dessert with me—in that Eucharistic moment we observed together in silence—I knew it was God in the guise of a little girl who quietly untied the knots in my heart. It was God who forgave me and gave my life back to me.

With a swipe across the head with a heavy book bag, Joyce taught me that all choices in life come with consequences from which we cannot escape. But it was the Twinkie broken in two that spoke of a sweeter, more gracious truth: At every turn, God is there, mysteriously loving us, forgiving us, helping us to mend our ways. We come to God with our arms outstretched, and in our frailty and tears we come to resemble the One who was crucified. It is to repentant thieves and other sinners that the gates of paradise swing wide open, that very same day.

The Good Son

When I was working as a priest in a parish in downtown Portland, I got to know a man named Abel Gonzales. We became fast friends for a number of reasons. First, he was an Oakland A's fan. This, of course, endeared him to me. What drew us together, however, was our love for this little hole-in-the-wall pub called The Tugboat Brewing Company, located on a little alley of a street called Ankeny. It occupied the space directly across the street from The Church of Elvis and shared a wall with Mary's Club, the oldest strip bar in Oregon. I oftentimes went to the Tugboat on my day off for a pint and a little peace and quiet. It was our A's caps that gave us permission to move from nod to hello to conversation. But it was our love for story that bound Abel and me in friendship.

I only knew him from our chats at the Tugboat. We never bumped into each other, never invited each other to our homes, never imagined or expected, I suppose, that our friendship would breathe any air other than that which carried the aroma of hops and barley. Of all the yarns he wove, there is one I will never forget. He must have told the story a dozen times, adding, subtracting, and enhancing details with poetic flurry. In retelling it here, I can still see Abel's eyes twinkle and mist, hear his measured voice. Though this is his story, it belongs to all of us.

❀ ❀ ❀ ❀ ❀ ❀ ❀

Before he stepped onto the bus, Abel gazed at the thermometer swinging from a rusty nail poked into the side of a Coca Cola machine a few feet away. One hundred and three degrees in the shade. It was then, as Abel boarded what could easily pass for a tin can with a transmission, while instinctively making the sign of the cross, that he knew this truly was going to be the bus ride from hell.

He was leaving sleepy Alturas, California, where he had spent the better part of a year living in a small room attached to the back of a filling station. At night he would fall asleep on his cot to the smell of gas and motor oil, with slivers of light piercing the wooden slats of the wall, illuminations of neon lights and passing automobile headlights. He was making his way back to Portland, Oregon, around three hundred miles up the road. He had left his home twelve months before in the middle of the night, hitchhiking all the way. He slept those first few days in tool sheds and barns and made do with the thirty bucks he was able to lift from his mom's purse not long after she had cried herself to sleep the night he departed.

To throw off the scent for the hound dogs sure to follow, Abel scribbled a quick note to his mother, telling her he was fine and that he would call her sometime. He gave the letter to a truck driver passing through and asked him to mail it when he got to San Francisco. Slamming the

Familiar faces and voices and homespun smells comforted him when the phantoms came out at night, and they held his wounded heart in warm embrace until the next sunrise.

hood of his truck shut, the man in overalls wiped his sweaty brow, cast a wary eye at the bony frame before him, and tossed the envelope into the cab of his truck. The big rig kicked up a good storm of dust as it pulled out of the station, leaving the young boy hacking and coughing, immersing him into the dry waters of a July Alturas baptism.

In the months that followed, Abel pumped gas and hid from Oregon license plates. He survived on hamburgers at the diner washed down with gulps of chocolate milk. Patches of free time found Abel reading true crime magazines, smoking cigarette stubs, and hanging out at the bowling alley, giving others the impression that he was fine and that nothing bothered him much at all.

When nighttime came, however, the ghosts would come and haunt him with memories of the life he left behind. He saw his younger sister standing right in front of him with the same sarcastic smile she always gave him and laughed aloud at how he could love and hate one person so much. He saw his tired mother asleep in front of the television set, a wizened old woman hopelessly ill-equipped to deal with the volcanic eruptions of her sixteen-year-old boy, but whose love he never really doubted.

Familiar faces and voices and homespun smells comforted him when the phantoms came out at night, and they held his wounded heart in warm embrace until the next sunrise. One morning, Abel awoke early, crying for no apparent reason. He got up out of bed, took one good look at himself in the chunk of mirror hanging from the bedpost, and decided it was time to go home.

❁ ❁ ❁ ❁ ❁ ❁ ❁

He made his way to the back of the bus where two seats lay vacant. Plopping himself into the one next to the window and placing a back-pack on the one next to the aisle, he began to pray over and over with the piety of a monk a prayer I imagine most everyone who has ever ridden on a bus has prayed one time or another: "O, PLEASE, DEAR GOD IN HEAVEN, please let there be enough seats on this bus so I won't have to sit next to anyone!" Slowly the bus began to fill.

One seat remained vacant, the one on which Abel's backpack lay. Beads of sweat collected on his forehead as he concentrated on the bus driver's hand, the one that held the lever that shut the front door. The engine began to cough and stutter and stammer to life, like morning lungs after a nighttime of smoking. As the door was being shut, a big, fleshy, hairy hand pierced the opening, catching the door just in time. Alarms sounded in Abel's head. "Don't open it, for God's sake!" he screamed silently. "Just leave! She can catch the next bus!"

Instead, a living, breathing, panting nightmare (as far as Abel was concerned) waddled down the aisle, as happy as could be, to the only empty seat left on the bus. A lady clutching the biggest purse Abel had ever laid eyes on, with wads of Kleenex stuffed into the short sleeves of her cotton dress and a "Jesus Loves You!" button pinned to her lapel, lowered herself into the seat next to Abel, letting gravity do most of the work.

A black cloud descended upon Abel; for a split second he entertained the possibility of catching the next bus. But the Greyhound began to pull out, and so he heaved a heavy sigh and lowered his head instead. A quick turn to the right out of the terminal jolted Abel's head toward the woman, and it landed softly on her exposed left arm. Pasted to the sweat of that arm, for the briefest of moments, Abel took in the whiff of sweet talcum, a scent so powerful in Abel's olfactory world that it rivaled church incense in sacredness. It was the scent of his mother. Somehow it made the mountain of flesh sitting next to him more human. Exhausted and blessed with incense talcum, Abel fell fast asleep.

He, along with everyone else on the bus, was awakened at around two in the morning by the blood-curdling scream of the colicky baby across the aisle. Overhead lamps were flicked on. The sounds of slumbering bodies emerging from bus hibernation trickled up and down the aisle. Pained expressions etched on tired faces ebbed, only to be replaced with a kind of choking frustration as the infant gave no hint of stopping any time soon.

The bus lumbered down the dark highway. Abel, crick-necked and sweaty and smelly, began to pray as if he had never prayed before. When he was younger and brash and irreverent, he used to secretly dismiss as contemptible those old ladies who fingered their rosary beads on buses and said grace in diners. Now he was whittling off Hail Mary's one after the other, hoping against hope that God would forget that he had been so neglectful of his religion and see fit to throw a little mercy his way. Across the aisle the young mother, having exhausted every known method of comforting, slumped in her seat, totally defeated by the screaming bundle on her lap.

The woman sitting next to Abel was unfazed. She reached over the aisle and gently took the demon child into her own arms, held it close to her breast, and caressed it with a love that startled Abel by its utter tenderness. It struck him as an ancient love, an icon of grace, the hand of God reaching across time and space, ushering home from the cold of night, as He had done so often before, yet another weary traveler, yet another lost child. The woman next to Abel began to sing a sweet lullaby, and the melody, soft and downy, wrapped itself around the baby and coaxed it to sleep.

✤ ✤ ✤ ✤ ✤ ✤ ✤

The song echoed in the long chamber of Abel's memory until he remembered, with a jolt, that this was the lullaby his own mother would whisper to him when thunderstorms shook his bed and monsters emerged from his closet at night. "Sleep, my baby, near to me.... Lu, lu, lu-lu, lu.... Close your velvet eyes." Abel stared out the window and onto a world draped in silence, and he fought back the tears. Hurt nurtured over many years melted away as the bus negotiated the turning, twining road cut through the mountains blanketed by pine trees and Douglas fir. Abel stole a glance at the woman sitting next to him, her eyes now closed, humming ever so sweetly. He studied her face for the first time, for he knew now it was God sitting next to him, or at the very least one of God's angels. He saw the face of a mother, delicate and fierce, eyes closed in peace, with lines of love etched around them. If they were anything like the rings on a tree, Abel thought to himself, then he was looking at a woman who, like God, had loved for a long, long time.

A new heart was given to Abel that long night, one sprinkled with sweet talcum, one that beat with new hope born of lullaby. He now knew he was going home to mend the heart of his mother, and that truth was almost too powerful for him to bear.

We of Christian sensibility would say that for Abel, the "good" son, the lofty mountains of pride and anger were made low and the age-old depths of despair and hurt were filled that morning on the bus. We would see that the road from Alturas to Portland was straight and level, paved with mercy, leading Abel from exile to a mother's embrace, into arms that are strong enough to tame the most ferocious of storms and tender enough to hold us in peace.

✤ ✤ ✤ ✤ ✤ ✤ ✤

Whenever I'm back in Portland, I make a point of stopping by The Tugboat Brewing Company ("45 latitude, 132 longitude, beer drinking conditions: always perfect") in the hope that Abel might be there. I haven't seen him in years, but I always have a Tugboat Ale in his honor and, in my own way, thank him. His story reminds me that God has a story to tell, too, and He's going to tell it. It has everything to do with the human journey and divine mercy, and how, at some point, they converge. It's a great tale of adventure. And of homecoming.

God Alone

When I want to be alone, I usually go to a baseball game or a bookstore or a pub or a movie house. When I want to be alone, I want to be around people. This may seem odd, but if you are of a gregarious nature, as I am, you know exactly what I'm talking about. It's not that we extroverts are afraid of being alone. It's just that for people of our stripe there is something about the steady flow of humanity, the hum of the public conversation, the heartbeat of the world that draws us, like bees to honey, into that same studied introspection our introverted counterparts find in solitary walks on deserted beaches.

❋ ❋ ❋ ❋ ❋ ❋ ❋

That is not to say that I cannot spend extended periods of time by myself. When I was a lad of five or six, I informed my mother and father one late summer morning that I was running away from home, having found fault in their parenting and disappointment in the dearth of affection from my brothers and sisters. It would be better, I told them in so many words, that I go it alone.

I was no fool, however. I had no intention of roaming the streets of our small town exposed to every two-bit thug, bully, and wino I might happen to bump into. Knowing my luck, that old, yellow-skinned lady that lived at the end of our street who had the permanent stink of bathroom disinfectant on her would probably kidnap me and force me into domestic servitude. No, Mama didn't raise an idiot. I slapped a few sandwiches together, raided the cookie jar, and whistled Dixie as I walked out the front door waving goodbye to my parents, brothers, and sisters. I was going to give them a good scare.

I scurried around the house and scampered unnoticed through the open window of my bedroom and, with a muffled giggle, slipped under my bed. It must have been around eleven in the morning. By noon I had consumed my peanut butter and jelly sandwiches and cookies. By twelve-thirty I was fast asleep. When I awoke, nary a shadow graced the room. It was completely dark except for the sliver of light below the door that opened out onto the hallway. Upstairs I could hear my mother and father talking to someone. I caught only snippets: "four feet tall," "brownish-red hair," "freckles," "a white T-shirt and blue jeans." My God, they were describing me! I climbed out from under the bed and cracked the door ever so slightly. Sure enough, upstairs at the kitchen table, my mother and father and my brothers and sisters were talking to two sheriff's deputies! I looked up above the stove and could see that it was eight o'clock. I had been under that bed for close to nine hours.

Being the youngest brother and seventh of nine kids, well, let me say that even back then I knew you couldn't *buy* that kind of exposure. I was Tom Sawyer enjoying from the church rafters his own funeral. I could see the worried lines drawn upon my mother's face, my father's chiseled jaw quivering ever so slightly. And, best of all, I could see my brothers and sisters, each registering on their somber faces alarm and dread and not, thank God, joyful relief. They were all imagining life without me and finding it wanting.

When I made my presence known (after the deputies departed), I was showered with kisses from my mother and father and embraced with hugs from my siblings. I got the spanking of my life later that night, when I confessed to my parents where I had been, but honestly it was worth it. I now knew that I was loved and would never be forgotten, and I didn't even have to run away from home to find that out.

❊ ❊ ❊ ❊ ❊ ❊ ❊

There is a Trappist Monastery outside of Louisville, Kentucky, tucked away in the blue grass hills, named Gethsemane. Three years ago I made the trip from Chicago to Gethsemane, arriving on December 28. Seven days. No *New York Times*, no ESPN Sports Center, no e-mail, cell phone, or Internet. No shopping malls, supermarkets, traffic jams, or running into students or their parents at the Cineplex ("So, Father, what movie are *you* seeing?").

I have to admit, it looked pretty darn good on paper: seven days of peace and quiet, a time to read and pray and rest and recharge the jets. Such thoughts sustained me as I traveled the Indiana Turnpike and cut a winding path through the rolling hills of southern Indiana and northern Kentucky. It was when I turned left onto Highway 247, beyond the Kwik Mart in tiny Culverton, Kentucky, that I began to entertain a different, more ominous notion about my impending week at the monastery. It dawned on me, as I drove through its front gate, that the Abbey of Gethsemane was named after the garden where Jesus spent a lonely night sweating and panting and weeping and wondering—in cries that only his Abba could hear—about why he had to face alone the suffering and humiliation of the Cross that he now most assuredly knew would be his.

It was when I passed through the private gate that only the monks of the Abbey were permitted to use and saw carved into the tall stone wall above the gate two simple words—"God Alone"—that I began to be haunted by the thought that I had made a terrible mistake. I was like Frodo in Tolkien's *Lord of the Rings* when he, along with Pippin, Merry and Sam, reached the farthest corner of the Shire and steps, not without a little trepidation, into the great unknown. Of course, Frodo was entrusted with the task of saving Middle Earth from total annihilation, but if what Dag Hammarskjold wrote was true, that "the longest journey is the journey inward," my task now seemed no less daunting. I, too, was stepping into untrod territory. It was going to be God and me. It was the stupidest decision I have ever made. Or so I was thinking.

I was stepping into untrod territory.

It was going to be God and me.

It was the stupiest decision

I have ever made.

You see, when God gets us alone, either by human (stupid) choice or divine persistence (don't think that at this very moment God isn't hunting you down), He will touch our hearts with a love that is, to be frank, dangerous. When it becomes God and me alone or God and you alone, there's no place to hide anymore. The truth must and does come out. For seven days it was God Alone. I told a few friends later that it was just God and me, *mano a mano*, a Spanish phrase which implies "hand-to-hand" combat. God and I went at it for seven days. And that is why—at least on one level—it was really crazy of me to go to Gethsemane in the first place. In the end, it was no contest. God won.

I couldn't run and hide. God had me cornered for seven days. I asked Him, sometimes begged Him, to leave me alone, but He wasn't listening to any of that. No, Jesus' Abba, my Abba, kept unpeeling my hands from my face, kept looking at me with piercing eyes, kept saying, "I love you," hoping, I suppose, that if He said it enough times I might believe Him.

I gave God in those first few days every reason I could think of why I was unworthy of such love, why it would be best if He went away and left me to myself. I'll spare you the long list, but suffice it to say, the list was apparently not long enough. St. Catherine of Siena had visions borne of such brutal quarrels with the Almighty, and she wrote those conversations down. According to Catherine, God once said to her, "My mercy is incomparably greater than all the sins anyone could commit," and that admission, that divine confession, is not only true, it is dangerous.

God's mercy changes everything. Every relationship in this world, especially those calibrated by the measuring sticks of power, position, or wealth is forever changed. Indeed, every relationship—including our relationship with God—is transformed by divine mercy predicated on sacrificial love. Jesus survived that dark and agonizing night in the Garden of Gethsemane, when his soul was "sorrowful, even unto death," because he believed that this love had no rival. He went to his death believing it; and our world has never been the same because Jesus trusted the power of his Abba's love. In the end, the world would come to see what Jesus felt in his broken heart that night in the garden, what his cross would come to signify for those who dared to believe, and what might very well have been the first thought Jesus had when the rock was rolled away from the tomb on the third day: The greatest expression of love in this world is mercy.

❖ ❖ ❖ ❖ ❖ ❖ ❖

When Nelson Mandela emerged from his jail cell on Robben Island after twenty-seven years of solitary confinement, he walked arm-in-arm with his white jailer, who over many of those years treated the future president of South Africa and Nobel Peace Prize winner with utter contempt and cruelty. Mandela chose to forgive, and he even invited his jailer to stand next to him a few years later when he was inaugurated president of their country. Revenge and retribution surrendered to truth and reconciliation; and a nation was saved from a bloodbath. After twenty-seven years of prison solitude, a man emerged, as from a tomb, transformed.

In a careless moment, when we accidently leave the door to our hearts slightly ajar, God comes barging in and corners us and tells us the truth that strips all the lies and deceptions and pretensions away: We are loved to the core of our being. We are loved despite all of our weaknesses and failures, and we are not going to change God's mind about this matter. Nor are we going to change His heart. The only question left for us to answer is this: Will we accept God's mercy?

Our lonely hearts will take us to the place we need to go. It may take awhile to get there; detours abound. And sometimes it seems we go kicking and screaming, resisting all the way. In the end, we know it is an unfair fight. "For God alone my soul waits in silence," the psalmist sings in Psalm 62. "He alone is my rock and my salvation, my fortress; I shall never be shaken."

TWO

The Deep Sea
The Power of Compassion

I called to the Lord out of my distress,
and he answered me;
out of the belly of Sheol I cried,
and you heard my voice.
You cast me into the deep,
into the heart of the seas,
and the flood surrounded me;
all your waves and your billows passed over me.
Then I said, "I am driven away from your sight;
how shall I look again upon your holy temple?"
The waters closed in over me;
the deep surrounded me;
weeds were wrapped around my head
at the roots of the mountains.
I went down to the land
whose bars closed upon me forever;
yet you brought up my life from the Pit,
O Lord my God.
As my life was ebbing away,
I remembered the Lord.

Jonah 2

The Watery Part of the World

There's nothing like the edge of the seashore to hush a human to wistful silence. A saturated strand of sand that hugs the ocean coaxes us to its grainy lip so that we might peer into the abyss and walk away humbled. It's easy to see why our ancestors were convinced that sea serpents and monsters lurked in its watery depths, or why, since we began to put thought to poetry and then ink to paper, the untamed sea has forever captured the human imagination. From Homer's Odysseus to Melville's Ishmael, the human story has been in part a tale of being drawn to the sea by its utter contradictions.

Teeming with life and yet violent unto death, the ocean is always quick to remind us that it is both cradle and grave. All earthly life, biologists tell us, emerged from its primordial soup billions of years ago. *In the beginning*, Genesis tells us, *the earth was a dark abyss, a wind-swept ocean*. Science and religion join hands at the seaside: This is where it all began. We traverse it at our peril, this ocean, so unpredictable and unforgiving in its demeanor. It blankets nearly three quarters of the earth's surface; it keeps us cool in the summer and warm in the winter. When calm and demure, it cups a boat like a mother her baby, and yet it will, without a second thought, swallow those of us who gave up our gills.

❋ ❋ ❋ ❋ ❋ ❋ ❋

E. E. Cummings once wrote, "For whatever we lose (like a you or a me), / It's always ourselves we find in the sea." Twenty years ago or so, I was with some friends at Cannon Beach on the Central Coast of Oregon. It was a cool September late afternoon. My friends had gone into town to procure a couple bottles of Willamette Valley wine, a wedge of Tillamook cheddar, and a box of crackers. I stayed behind, reading my book as the sun was beginning to set. Haystack Rock, a 235-foot-tall basalt monolithic crag, rested peacefully in the tide pool fifty feet away. Terns and puffins circled the rock lazily.

Dad and Grandma (my mother's mom) had died the previous year; and the previous June Mom had been diagnosed with lung cancer. While all my brothers and sisters rallied around our mother, determined to buck her up with words of hope and determination, I, the Catholic seminarian, was having a very hard time wrapping my mind around the whole thing. God and I were barely on speaking terms. And when I did talk to Him, I didn't shy away from the harsh word, the damning phrase. As I began to cry, the tears—each one carrying a bit of rage—burned my cheeks.

When we get a glimpse of eternity,

we never forget it.

I remember now the first thoughts of Ishmael in Melville's *Moby Dick* and how perfectly they fit my mood back then: "Whenever I find myself growing grim about the mouth; whenever it is a damp, drizzly November in my soul; whenever I find myself involuntarily pausing before coffin warehouses, and bringing up the rear of every funeral I meet; and especially whenever my hypos get such an upper hand of me, that it requires a strong moral principle to prevent me from deliberately stepping into the street, and methodically knocking people's hats off—then, I account it high time to get to sea as soon as I can."

I began to walk the beach, and as I did my heart drifted to "the watery part of the world" as Ishmael called it, for the solace and the hint of hope it might afford me. The water lapped at my feet and the horizon touched the shadow of the earth and kissed the soft red hue of Venus' Belt. It was all quite beautiful, and for a moment I was thankful for the simple gift it was.

I passed an old man still lounging in his wicker chair on the sand. A thick wool blanket hugged him all the way up to his chin; soft white strands of his thinning hair floated in the breeze. His eyes were closed, and his lips formed a very sweet smile. I stood there for a moment and stared at him, not really caring if he caught me spying. Actually I secretly wished he had, for in a gracious act of mercy God gave me a glimpse of eternity, and it seemed a real shame not to share it with someone.

You see, when I gazed upon this cocooned and wrinkly-faced cod-ger, I could see him as he once was: a young lad, facing the dawn and not the sunset, his whole life ahead of him, dressed in wool knickers and argyle socks, and, as the young are wont to do, dreaming great dreams. Knowing how time has a way of bending us under its weight, how it can dry the body out and make bones brittle, I observed this old man and marveled at the resiliency of the soul. How could someone so old appear so young?

When we get a glimpse of eternity, we never forget it. It has a way of softening the sharp edges of anger and reassuring the troubled heart, and when we bump into an eternal moment, as I did along the seashore, it reminds us that as old as the ocean may be, it is still a wee infant in the arms of God.

The ocean is vast and deep; it is unbridled and wild and terrifying, really. But when viewed at sunset on a calm September Oregon evening, it is mostly reassuring. Henry Wordsworth said the ocean is "a mighty harmonist," and he was right. One early evening years ago, the watery part of the world hushed the cries of my heart and sang for me her grand and ancient song, as if for the first time. Some things, the ocean crooned, last forever.

That's the Deal

T he first time I remember meeting Nick Madrid I was at the Niles Bowling Alley on Milwaukee Avenue, north of the Chicago city limits. He was waiting for the ball return to spit out his rock after having rolled a 7-10 split—"bedposts" as toilers in the trade call it. His teammates were shouting words of encouragement as Nick shot them the look of calm determination found only on the faces of serious bowlers when facing the formidable 7-10 split. Nick was a serious bowler. You could tell by looking at his bowling shoes: worn and tired looking, just the way you want them. Nick carefully toweled off his ball, slid into position on the runway, second arrow from the right, and waited his turn. His shoulders lifted and lowered as he took one long breath. No way Nick was going to settle for knocking down just one pin. He had been working on a perfect game—a "four bagger" already was achieved, but now in the fifth frame he was facing old snake eyes.

Nick pushed away, made his way down the lane, and released a real looper. The ball took the scenic route, curving purposefully to the edge of the left gutter, where with a little luck it would kiss the far edge of the 7-pin before diving off the cliff, thus propelling the pin sideways, where it would bump into the 10-pin and make the spare.

The ball, however, midway down the lane, corrected itself and split the uprights. All the body English in the world could not save the frame for Nick. Turning around and returning to his seat, his earlier look of determination was replaced with a look of surprise. He had fully expected to pick up the split. A thousand-to-one odds, easy, and Nick had already pictured it in his mind. Taking a long, lazy sip from his Coke, Nick accepted the condolences of his teammates, the Pin Dons as they were called, and began to cheer on the next bowler dressed in Notre Dame green and white. "Let's get a strike *now*," Nick shouted out. He may have lost the battle, but he wasn't going to lose the war.

Nick was a sophomore then. The next time our paths crossed in a definitive way was almost two years later in the halls of Notre Dame High School. It was the last day of classes, the day the seniors gleefully performed their annual prank. I implored the seniors I had taught that year not to do anything that would cause damage to any property. The previous year a number of seniors super-glued the locks of a couple of dozen classroom doors. Replacing those locks cost several thousand dollars. I suggested more benign shenanigans. One year for instance, a group of seniors released three little pigs into the school. One had the number "1" painted on its back; the second, the number "2"; and the third, the number "4." The principal, dean, janitor, and several seniors drafted into service apparently spent the better part of the morning and early afternoon hunting down the non-existent third pig, much to the delight of most everyone who was aware of the ruse.

I arrived at my classroom that last day of school at six-thirty in the morning, relieved to find that my key fit the lock. It was eerily quiet around the school. Students began to fill the halls, and the first period began without a hitch. Clearly the seniors were attempting to lure us into a false sense of security. Second period commenced and concluded. Still nothing. Teachers shot glances back and forth to each other during the change in classes. Batten down the hatches, we were saying to each other with our eyes. Katie, bar the door. A quiet storm's a brewin'.

I had fifth period free; and sometimes I used that time to get a little fresh air, so I was walking down the hallway that led to the somewhat secluded service entrance to the cafeteria. That's where I encountered Nick and two of his comrades. They were in the process of releasing a dozen fully grown ducks from their cardboard box containers. His compatriots sensed my impending presence and took full advantage by bolting out the door. Nick, however, was not looking up when I arrived on the scene. He was too busy trying to pull one of the ducks out of the box as quietly as possible.

He stood up holding a very unhappy duck in his hands when I was around ten yards away. Our eyes met, and you would have thought by looking at him that he had just encountered Jesus Christ at the second coming.

"Quack," said the duck.

"Busted," I said.

"Damn!" Nick said.

❀ ❀ ❀ ❀ ❀ ❀ ❀

Nick graduated on time and began his studies at a local university. I got a call one afternoon from his mother, Emily, asking if I might come by and see Nick. He had not been feeling well the past couple of months and had agreed to see the doctor. He underwent a series of tests and was subsequently diagnosed with leukemia. So when I approached the Madrid's front door that afternoon, I half-expected to see Nick connected to IV's and hidden behind a pallid complexion.

"Father Pat, come on in!" Nick said as he ushered me into his home. We shook hands. I couldn't help but noticed that he looked exactly as he had when I first saw him at the bowling alley a few years back. He had already steeled himself for battle and was looking beyond the minor setback of a 7-10 split. There was the same goofy smile, the same glimmer in his eyes. It didn't take long for the old stories to surface, and we happily replayed that fateful day with the ducks. We walked out to his garage so he could show off his new car: a late-model black Trans Am with a deep rich red interior. And he showed me pictures of a recent cruise he had enjoyed with some close friends. Of course, most of the shots were of him and a lovely young woman he had met and fallen head-over-heels for.

Cancer never came up that first day, which was fine. I remember telling him I would be keeping him in my prayers and that if he would like I would be more than happy to stop by again. He said that would be great.

❀ ❀ ❀ ❀ ❀ ❀ ❀

Nick and I spent four or five more afternoons together over the next number of months, sometimes in his living room, sometimes in his room at the University of Chicago Hospital while he was undergoing chemotherapy or tests. Same determined look, same glimmer in his eyes. But he was changing. He was no longer a teenager. He carried himself like a battle-hardened warrior, undeterred now by low white blood cell counts or infections or fatigue. And we talked more about God and faith and the questions that come at night when no one is around.

One day Emily called and asked if I might come down to the hospital. Nick was taking oxygen now through a mask, unable really to breathe on his own. I arrived at around midnight. Emily and Nick's father, Narcisso, were there, as they were every single day. Nick was conscious, but clearly his body was ready to give out. We sat together for a little while.

Sitting with Nick's parents

brought me reluctantly

to that place in the human heart

where joy and sorrow kiss.

Nick thanked me for coming. I thanked him for letting me. I asked him if he needed anything, anything at all, and he shook his head. I asked if he wanted to be anointed, and he nodded. So as a new day came, Emily and Narcisso and I stood around Nick's bed and prayed for him. We laid our hands on him and spoke words of comfort and courage. I anointed his forehead and the palms of his hands, and together we all prayed the Lord's Prayer. Emily wept; Narcisso remained calm and composed, even as tears welled up in his eyes. I said good night to Nick and told him that I would be praying for him. I left the room pretty choked up: Seeing Nick there smiling, with tears streaming down his cheeks, was almost too much for me to bear.

❁ ❁ ❁ ❁ ❁ ❁ ❁

Emily and Narcisso invited me to their home on the first anniversary of Nick's death. We sat around their dining room table and celebrated mass and afterwards opened a bottle of wine. Sitting with Nick's parents that evening brought me reluctantly to that place in the human heart where joy and sorrow kiss. I recalled in my own mind the verbal etchings of grief uttered by C. S. Lewis at the end of William Nicholson's play *Shadowlands*. Lewis was trying to make sense of the untimely death of his wife, Joy. "Why love, if losing hurts so much?" he asked. "I have no answers anymore: only the life I have lived…. The pain now is part of the happiness then. That's the deal."

Emily and Narcisso spoke of the love they had for Nick in the present tense. I imagine to this day they still do. Love survived, although it hurt and left them deeply wounded. In fact, I was convinced that the wound would never be healed. How could it? But that was part of the deal.

The night Nick died, Emily told me, she was alone with him for a short while. "His eyes opened, and he looked over at me," she said. "He patted the side of his bed, telling me in the only way he could that he wanted me to sit next to him on the bed. So I did. I sat right next to him. At one point he took my head into his arms and placed my head upon his chest. Father, he kept it there for ten minutes. He held me there for ten minutes. And I kept telling him, I love you, Nicky."

❁ ❁ ❁ ❁ ❁ ❁ ❁

And now, every so often, when I open my Bible to retrieve a scripture verse or to pray or study, Nick's picture falls out. I gaze upon the face of a young man in his graduation pose, brimming with youthful confidence and—if you look closely enough—the nascent courage of a warrior. I'll call to mind the night he went to God, when in his last hour, he reached out with ineffable mercy to the mother who had years ago cradled him in her arms as a newborn but who now rested in his. And I remember once again that love—fierce and mighty and unrelenting—has no rival. It gives us permission to face unimaginable suffering unafraid.

A mother holds her son at the foot of a cross planted on a hill outside the gates of Jerusalem one dark Friday afternoon. A son holds her mother in his arms in a Chicago hospital room at the hour of his death. The last word in both cases was the same. It is love. That's the deal.

All Over but the Cryin'

I was six years old. It was the summer after my kindergarten year, a hot, hazy, lazy July afternoon, the kind of day where long gulps of Coca Cola never tasted so good. I was with my family at Knowland Park Zoo in Oakland enjoying a picnic. From a distance, we must have appeared so normal: girls in play dresses and boys in Levi's and white T-shirts tossing a football and slinging a Frisbee; Dad lying across one of the blankets splayed out on the tall grass, his head resting in the lap of his wife, who is reading one of her romance novels; Grandma in her lawn chair sipping iced tea and swatting flies and surveying it all from her septuagenarian perch.

Actually, the girls hated those dresses but had to wear them because Mom had bought them at a discount and got a kick out of all the girls wearing the same dress. (Secretly she wished we were the Von Trapp family.) The boys were in fact tossing a football, but God help you if you dropped it. We devised the game right then and there: You drop the ball and you got punched in the arm later. Brian, the eldest, kept a rather dubious count. Dad was sleeping because he was plain exhausted; he's all of thirty-six years old and already a father of nine. And the book Mom was reading? I bet it was a home repair manual on how to fix a garbage disposal. It's amazing what a good, sturdy garbage disposal can grind up if one is patient enough. And indeed, Grandma was sipping her iced tea peacefully, enjoying the view. That much was true.

❋ ❋ ❋ ❋ ❋ ❋ ❋

I was six years old, and I was learning already that nothing—or pretty much nothing—is what it appears to be. Most of the time, for instance, I didn't know if I loved my brothers and sisters or hated them. Walk by the Hannon house on any given day and you'd probably hear someone screaming bloody murder or glass breaking or one argument heating up as another was simmering down. If you were the playground bully at Our Lady of Grace, you might even conclude that one of the runts of the Hannon litter would be easy pickings, lacking, it would appear, the necessary familial bonds to protect one's rear flank. But you would be wrong. Our school was comprised of fierce clans: the Clancys and the Quinns and the Boyces and the Hallorans; and we Hannons were among the fiercest. While the nuns desperately tried to inculcate Christian values and promote a code of behavior that transcended tribal loyalties, playground justice was swift and uncompromising, predicated as it was on a very simple dictum: You mess with one of us, you mess with all of us.

One of the last fights I ever got into was with a classmate who disparaged Julie's reputation. Now, I had disparaged my little sister's reputation hundreds of times in the comfort of our own home—such was my prerogative—but I would be damned if anyone else was going to drag my sister's good name through the mud. (Incidentally, Julie finked on me to Sister Maria Del Carmen later that day, not with any malicious intent, but simply because she was so excited about the fight that she wanted everyone to know.)

In the end, I accepted the fact that I loved and hated my siblings with equal intensity, and that was the way of the world. This made me at a young age a little more discerning of people. I believed then that most of us are basically good, and I still do. But we're not unlike sleeping volcanoes. On the outside we are as we appear: majestic and stunning, cutting dignified poses against the backdrop of a soft sky. But beneath the surface there is boiling, roiling lava: passion and paroxysm and prickly pride ready to be released. The hidden within wields great power precisely because of its dormant, quiescent nature. When it does see the light of day, it usually leaves in its wake utter devastation.

✿ ✿ ✿ ✿ ✿ ✿ ✿

It's late afternoon. The fried chicken and potato salad have been eaten, and Dad is stirring. The brothers are lounging around burping and sighing heavily, like lions after they have polished off their prey and sucked the bones dry. The girls are off to the see the monkeys at the zoo. Mom is enjoying a rare moment of placidity, while Grandma sits in her lawn chair sipping iced tea and humming a tune. I decide to explore a bit, hoping to step beyond the range of my mother's voice so I can honestly say I didn't hear her when she bellows for her brood at sundown.

I emerge from a thick grove of trees that spills out onto a large expansive meadow. Mom remembered wild horses grazing in that field when she was a child, but now it is cordoned off by a tall chain-linked fence that keeps mustangs and picnickers alike away.

And there they are: a mother and father about the age of my own parents, snarling at a young black boy about my age. The man is having such a conniption that his baseball cap falls off his head. Spit is flying everywhere. Clinging to the woman from behind is, as far as I could tell, their own boy, a blonde-haired kid in shorts. I'm at least a hundred yards away and could still *see* the kid shaking, as if he were clinging to the mast of a ship on a violent sea, convinced that if he ever let go he would be tossed into the abyss.

The hidden within wields great power precisely because of its dormant, quiescent nature.

The man and the woman each grab an arm of the little black boy. The blonde-haired boy shuffles along, refusing to let go of his mother's leg. The father, with his free hand, grabs the arm of his son and shoves him forward so that the two boys are facing each other.

"Hit the little nigger in the face," I hear the man say, and I begin to shake.

"Go ahead," the woman barks, "do as your father says." The little black boy is crying. The little white boy is crying, his hands covering his face. And now I'm crying. Their son shakes his head. He refuses. And now the man shakes his son and says, "You hit this nigger in the face now or you'll get the hiding of your life when you get home."

I'm horrified and frightened, having never witnessed such evil before in my life, and now I'm clinging to the trunk of a tree, hoping to God they don't see me. I have no idea what precipitated the ugly drama unfolding before me, but now I am petrified that my snooping could, if it were exposed, cause me bodily harm.

Finally, the little white boy forms a fist and plants it in the face of the little black boy. "One more time," the father says, and his son let's out a sobbing cry that echoes in the meadow, as if he is convinced that one more punch will destroy *him*. "We ain't leaving 'til you do it," says the father, and so the son obeys. Then the three walk away together, man and woman with son trailing three or four feet behind. The little black boy gets up and he's still crying. He brushes the grass and dirt from his shirt and pants as he begins to walk away. There is an opening into the woods twenty yards away from me and that's where he is heading. Ten feet or so before he disappears into the woods, my moving around makes the slightest noise and he stops in his tracks like an alarmed deer. He slowly turns his heard in my direction and our eyes meet. He sees me crying while I see him crying.

"Ain't no big deal," he says to me. But I know he is lying.

I race back to the park where my family is packing up. I run into my grandma's arms as she is still sitting in her lawn chair. No sense in her getting up until everyone is waiting for her in the car, I suppose, but I'm grateful because, more than anything else in the whole world, what I need at that moment are ancient arms to wrap around me and tell me that everything will be okay. I sob and sob into the cleavage of Grandma's bosom, coming up every so often for air. I never told her, or anyone else for that matter, what I had seen. She rocked me in her arms and whispered in my ear, "It's okay now, sweetheart. It's all over but the cryin', all over but the cryin'."

❖ ❖ ❖ ❖ ❖ ❖ ❖

Forty-years later, I'm still haunted by the memory of that late-afternoon in the meadow. I wonder what ever happened to that little black boy and that little white boy, both of them victims. I'm hoping that the black boy understood that in my sixth year of life, the only thing I had to give him—the only thing I could give him—were tears that matched his own. And I pray to God that the tears we three kids shed that day might someday be collected and mingle with all the tears that have ever been shed and form a mighty wave of salty water that will wash this world of ours and make it clean again.

A Gift for Brendan

Brendan sat by himself on the bus, gazing out onto the passing pastures and fields of crops. He looked too wise for his twelve years, as if he had seen too much of the darker side of the world for a boy who had not yet shaved. He carried with him a scar that ran down and across his right cheek, evidence of a fight he had gotten into the previous summer while coming home late from school.

It was June 24, 2000, and we were on our way to Hook Head, a tiny peninsula on the southeast coast of Ireland that is home to a medieval lighthouse, a thirteenth-century Norman tower that still sends a pulsing light out onto the Celtic Sea. Our group from Notre Dame High School in Niles, Illinois, had joined Sister Mairead and her group of Irish kids the previous day. Brendan and the nineteen other boys and girls lived on the outskirts of Dublin, a section of run-down, government-subsidized housing called Jobstown. Brendan, in his tight-lipped moodiness, was the exception to the rule, for these children of God boasted a vocabulary as salty as any sailor's and a lilt of laughter that could melt steel. These were tough kids who had already learned to negotiate the daily perils of life as they experienced them in their homes, their school, and on their streets. They were on this trip because they had, for the most part, kept their noses clean and their grades up. Like Jesus, few of them had traveled more than thirty miles from their front porches, and now here they were bouncing up and down a narrow dirt road a hundred kilometers from Dublin, weaving their way to Hook Head on the longest day of the year. As they say in Ireland, everything was "grand."

❖ ❖ ❖ ❖ ❖ ❖ ❖

"Mark, can I see your hat?"

Brendan, the silent one, had spoken. He spoke so softly that Mark, one of the Notre Dame students sitting across the aisle, didn't even hear him—or pretended not to. So Brendan poked Mark's ribs and asked again, "Mark, let's have a look at your hat." (Brendan had set his sights on that hat the second he had seen it when we arrived the previous day.

What he didn't know was that the blue and green Notre Dame cap was Mark's prized possession. If he were to take it off at all—and some of us suspected that at least in the summertime he never did—it would have to be surgically removed.)

You should have observed the unspoken conversation that transpired between Brendan and Mark. I think Mark would have given up either of his parents rather than his beloved cap. But if Brendan had given you the look he had given Mark, you would have surrendered the keys to your Lexus if he had asked for them. So Mark handed his cap to Brendan and Brendan secured it on his head, as if he had worn it every day of his life. For the rest of the day, Mark did not let Brendan or his cap out of his sight. I had the sneaking suspicion that Brendan was aware of this and didn't seem to mind at all.

For the next three days, the same drama played out: Brendan asking Mark if he could see his cap; Mark handing over the cap as if he were giving up both kidneys and a lung; Brendan wearing the cap all day with growing pride, never far from Mark's attentive lighthouse gaze; and then by evening, Brendan surrendering the cap to a relieved Mark.

❖ ❖ ❖ ❖ ❖ ❖ ❖

On a beautifully crisp summer day we all gathered at the shore of the bay, the gaggle of Irish boys and girls and "the Yanks," as we were affectionately called. We were going to spend the day kayaking, an activity I didn't know was indigenous or even common to the Irish. Then I remembered the Irish monks who paddled out seven miles off the western shore of Kerry on their way to their home on Skellig Michael back in the sixth century, and I admonished myself for my lapse of memory.

Everyone was excited about spending the day paddling around the rocky shoreline to the other side of the cape, where lunch would be waiting for us. People began to pair off. In the end there were only two left unpaired, Brendan, with Mark's Notre Dame cap on loan, and me.

"Well, what do you say, Brendan, shall we give it a go?" I asked.

Brendan was still in his street clothes; his head was down, his hands were deep in his pockets, and he was kicking rocks. The other Irish kids picked up the scent of his fear and began to rib him: "Ah, dear Brendan, you're a bit afraid of the water, are you, you poor child!" one of them said, and Brendan began to turn red. He went and sat on a rock away from the boys, but they came walking up to him and berated him a bit more.

"Don't be acting the maggot, Sean," Brendan said to the one closest to him, and you could tell by his tone that it was more a warning than a request. Brendan began muttering to himself. Sister Mairead called the other boys over to the shore, and they finished putting on their wet suits and life preservers. I told everyone to go on ahead, that I would stay with Brendan.

"So, what's going on, Brendan?" I asked.

Brendan remained silent, and tears began welling up in his eyes.

"Well, we can meet them over at the other side," I offered. "Everything will be okay."

"Father, I really don't know how to swim," Brendan explained. "Well, I *know* how to swim; it's just that I'm not particularly adept, you know?" I was impressed that he correctly used the word "adept" in the sentence.

"I'll tell you what, Brendan," I said. "We'll go together, and I promise you, you won't drown. We'll take it nice and slow." Brendan thought about it a bit, calculating the risk, and finally nodded his head.

It took us an hour longer than everyone else to get to the other side, but I'll tell you this, it wasn't because of Brendan. When it comes to kayaking, I discovered I had two left arms. Towards the end of our sojourn, Brendan, who had quickly figured out how to maneuver the kayak, was instructing me.

"Father, you're rowing too hard," he said. "See, the ore has got to just skim the surface. You're not very adept, are you now, Father?" He was wearing a playful grin for my pleasure.

"Don't be acting the maggot, Brendan," I said, and he laughed because he knew I didn't have clue about what I had just said.

❖ ❖ ❖ ❖ ❖ ❖ ❖

The day finally came when we had to say goodbye to Sister Mairead and the boys and girls from Jobstown. We all exchanged addresses and hugs and even a few tears. A group picture was taken on that drizzly, gray morning, and then another round of hugs and handshakes and promises were exchanged. Then it was time to leave. Brendan, of course, was wearing Mark's Notre Dame cap. Mark approached him slowly, and you could tell this was going to be a painful transaction. I half expected Brendan to bolt and run for the hills, but he stood there like a brave soldier waiting for the cigarette and the blindfold. Words were exchanged, and then a handshake. Finally, Mark reached to take his cap off Brendan's head.

In a world

of suffering and grief,

tears always surrender

to rejoicing.

Except instead of removing it Mark sort of patted it a few times and then adjusted its bill so that it sat correctly on Brendan's head.

Mark was the last one to get into the van before we left. He sat there in the back seat, as quiet as I had ever heard him. Looking at him in the rear view mirror, I saw not the face of sadness and loss I had expected but rather the face of utter peace, as if Mark had discovered some eternal truth about life and was slowly being transformed by it right before my eyes.

As for Brendan, he stood with the rest of the Irish boys and girls as they waved goodbye to us. He had the biggest grin on his face, for he was now the only kid in Jobstown with a Notre Dame High School baseball cap. He must have known that though time and distance would separate the two of them, he would never be far from Mark's watchful gaze; that is, if the heart has eyes, and I suspect that Brendan was beginning to believe that it does. I also think it didn't bother Brendan one bit to know that somewhere in North America someone was thinking of him and that he would never be forgotten by Mark, just as he would never forget his American friend.

I am reminded of the words of Shug Avery, a character in Alice

Walker's novel *The Color Purple*, when she tells her friend Celie matter of factly, "People think pleasing God is all God care about. But any fool living in the world can see It always trying to please us back."

I sometimes wonder if that was the truth Mark discovered the day we said goodbye to the children of Jobstown: the truth that mostly God just wants to "please us back." I suspect at the very least Mark got a hint of that truth that day, and it was given to him because he was open to receiving it. It was as if Mark's life to that point had been a preparation for one sacred transaction between him and an Irish kid from the Dublin projects. In the giving away of his most prized possession to a child who knew well the subtle art of seeking, asking, and knocking, Mark's human heart beat in time with the heart of God.

Maybe Mark began to understand what Jesus understood so well and what most of us spend a lifetime trying to believe: In a world of suffering and grief, tears always surrender to rejoicing.

THREE

The Desert Journey
The Cost of Mercy

O God, you are my God, I seek you,
my soul thirsts for you; my flesh faints for you,
as in a dry and weary land
where there is no water.
So I have looked upon you in the sanctuary,
beholding your power and glory.
Because your steadfast love is better than life,
my lips will praise you.
So I will bless you as long as I live;
I will lift up my hands and call on your name.
My soul is satisfied as with a rich feast,
and my mouth praises you with joyful lips
when I think of you on my bed,
and meditate on you in the watches of the night;
for you have been my help,
and in the shadow of your wings I sing for joy.
My soul clings to you;
your right hand upholds me.

Psalm 63

Rattlesnake Chili

I had been around hot before, but this was ridiculous. Eugene Jerome, the protagonist in Neil Simon's play "Biloxi Blues," said it perfectly when he was standing at attention along with the other army recruits absorbing the brutal midday heat of the Mississippi gulf coast: "Man it's hot," he said. "It's like Africa hot. Tarzan couldn't take this kind of hot." He could have very well been speaking of Indio, California, which may be fertile ground for growing dates and oranges and avocados and grapes—thanks to the Colorado River Aqueduct—but thirty seconds under its early afternoon sun and you knew it didn't matter how much they dressed it up or soaked it with river water: It was still the desert.

My friend Mike Jaeger and I had arrived in Indio, California, a week before the rest of our group from the University of Portland. The six of us came down at the invitation of Father Ned Reidy, a Holy Cross priest we had come to know at the university who was beginning new work at a college campus ministry center in the Coachella Valley. Ned thought it would be a good summer experience and enticed us with tales of long twilight desert evenings reclining under shaded date trees, and weekends resting beside cool oasis water sipping ice-cold lemonade, and falling asleep at night to the distant sounds of mariachi music and Latino love songs trickling out of passing pick-ups and transistor radios.

We were standing outside the Greyhound bus terminal waiting for Johnny and Alicia, our hosts for the summer, to pick us up. I was leaning against a thirty-foot-tall palm tree outside the front door and sweating like a pig. It was May 5, 1980, Cinco de Mayo, and there was a palpable sense of anticipation in the air. Cinco de Mayo commemorates the victory of five thousand ill-equipped Mestizo and Zapotec Indians, under General Ignacio Zaragoza, over the French army of Napoleon III in 1862 at the Battle of Puebla; but as far as Mike and I were concerned, it meant drinking ice-cold Cokes and feasting on chimichangas and tacos until our bellies burst. We already knew that Johnny and Alicia were taking us directly to Our Lady of Perpetual Help Catholic Church, where we were to be put to work setting up tables and chairs for the fiesta that night. We couldn't wait.

It had to have been a hundred-and-ten in the shade. Frying eggs on a greasy griddle, that's what it felt like, but Mike and I were taking it all in: the palm and date trees; the clear, dry air; the penetrating sun; the music; the smell of tortilla factories; the laid-back life embraced by the locals. Riding over to the church, Mike and I were sitting in the bed of a pick-up with Johnny and Alicia's eleven-year old daughter Jessica. She noticed we were both wearing flip-flops, our pink toes exposed; and she wanted to know where our socks were. With a sly wink my way, Mike explained to Jessica that folks from Oregon don't wear socks, ever. Jessica was flabbergasted. "Mom," she yelled through the sliding window to the cab, "they don't own any socks!" For the next three months, Mike and I decided not to wear the socks we packed, just to see the look on Jessica's face every day. This is going to be a great summer, I said to myself: a Beach Boy California Summer…without the beach.

✦ ✦ ✦ ✦ ✦ ✦

For that week before the rest of our group arrived, Mike and I worked in the bean fields. We got up around five in the morning and worked until three in the afternoon. Johnny and Alicia warned us to cover up while we were out there, but we were seduced by the siren song of the sun and wore T-shirts, shorts, and flip-flops instead. The migrant workers got a kick out of us; our pink backs bare to the wickedly hot sun, our soft white skin exposed. Mike and I openly wondered why they of brown skin would wear wide-rimmed hats, shirts with long sleeves, long khaki trousers, and boots. Three days in the sun and we would be bronzed gods for sure.

Stupid gringos. How do you say that in Spanish? I'm pretty sure that's what our fellow workers were whispering under their breath as we picked beans together. That first afternoon, Mike and I got burnt to a crisp. In retrospect, it is clear we hadn't thought it through completely, but at the time neither of us suspected we were in much danger. For a week, we spent the first part of every morning and the last part of every evening putting Noxzema moisturizing cream on each other's back. Every morning that week, when we hopped out of the truck at the bean field, we were met with applause from our fellow workers as they saw us dressed in long-sleeved shirts, khaki trousers, and wide-rimmed hats.

❀ ❀ ❀ ❀ ❀ ❀ ❀

Twenty-seven cents a bushel basket. That's what we were paid. It was back-breaking and boring work; even now I am incapable of painting it with even the palest of romantic hues. Picking beans in the desert for ten hours a day for pennies a bushel is sweaty, dreary work, any way you look at it. There was no shadow or shade, only the sun-bleached sky and the kind of heat that percolated the blood. Mike and I worked with fury, trying to keep up with the other pickers, but each of them filled three baskets to our one. They were working to put food on the table and clothes on their children and medicine into the stomachs of their mothers and fathers. We were soft college students from the north, without a care in the world.

We were humbled

by the quiet dignity

with which our compadres

went about eking out

an existence.

They were nimble of finger, alert, focused on the work at hand, driven by the desire not just to survive but to live. Mike and I, no slouches by anyone's definition, were humbled by the quiet dignity with which our compadres went about eking out an existence. I was beginning to understand why Ned was so insistent that we come down to the desert. Certainly I was beginning to see—under that uncompromising desert sun—things more clearly, more truthfully. Maybe Elvis was right when he said, "Truth is like the sun. You can shut it out for a time, but it ain't goin' away."

❀ ❀ ❀ ❀ ❀ ❀ ❀

On the fourth day, a rattlesnake snuck up on Mike and me as we were picking beans. I was exhausted and tired, three minutes from a heat stroke, and hadn't a clue that it was in fact *we* who were sneaking up on a rattler who was sunning himself and minding his own business. I was fantasizing about the six-pack of Corona waiting for us in the fridge back at Johnny and Alicia's. One of the workers heard the rattling, walked the twenty paces over to our row of beans, and with a shovel whacked the five-foot-long rattler senseless. He then cut off its head with a bowie knife and asked if I wanted the rattle. I said no, he should have it. And for the rest of our time in that bean field, this man would sneak up with that rattle and scare the bejeezus out of me, time after time. The chorus of warm and playful laughter that followed made me feel that somehow my fellow workers had adopted me as their brother. At least that is what I wanted to believe.

✦ ✦ ✦ ✦ ✦ ✦ ✦

On the seventh and last day in the field, the crew had a feast under the noon sun. The field manager let us knock off a few hours early, and so we congregated around one of the huge flatbed trucks we used to transport the bushels of green beans. We had beer on ice and plenty of southwestern chili, sopped up with soft corn tortillas. Rumor had it that it was rattlesnake meat in the chili, but I was never able to confirm it.

✦ ✦ ✦ ✦ ✦ ✦ ✦

The desert is such a forbidding place. On the surface it seems inhospitable to life and living, and yet it can, if we dare to venture there, help us to see what too often remains hidden in our lives. There is indeed a taxing quality to desert sun: It saps us of strength and strips us to the bare, whitewashed bone. And yet, there are blossoms in the desert: hearty, rugged, triumphant blossoms.

Life abounds in the desert, washed in sweat and dried by sun and wind. It is a dangerous place that can and does humble those of fragile constitution. St. Anthony of the Desert, a third-century anchorite, made the dry Egyptian desert his home, led there by the spirit of Jesus who spoke to him once, inviting him to sell all he had, leave it all behind, and follow the Lord. "I saw," Anthony once wrote, "the snares that the enemy spreads out over the world and I said groaning, 'What can get through from such snares?' Then I heard a voice saying to me, 'Humility.'"

It is hard, exacting labor, this work of humility: to accept and celebrate who God is and who we are and allow God to strip us to the bone so He can recreate within us hearts that are merciful and forgiving, minds that dare to imagine a life unencumbered by shame or guilt or grudge or sin.

On the seventh day there in the desert, we all rested in what little shade that flatbed truck could provide. There was a feast there: a feast of Corona beer and rattlesnake chili and singing and laugh lines etched on sun-baked skin. God was there, taking it all in, and yes, my fellow workers had adopted me as their brother.

Life abounds in the desert.

My Brother's Keeper

In his short story "A Child's Christmas in Wales," Dylan Thomas, the Welsh wordsmith, wrote, "It snowed last year too: I made a snowman and my brother knocked it down and I knocked my brother down and then we had tea." Dylan's words pretty much sum up the relationship I had with my brother Greg when we were young boys. Thirty-one months apart in age, a sister born between us, Greg and I spent a lot of time together. We shared a bedroom for sixteen years and the same bed for thirteen. That's a lot of face time when you take a step back and look at it. Snippets of memory paint an intimate picture of my brother and me.

Off and on during the 1960s, when Chet Huntley and David Brinkley co-anchored the "NBC Nightly News," Greg and I adopted their signature sign-off after turning off the bedroom lights and jumping under the covers: "Goodnight, Chet," I'd say. "Good Night, David," he'd say. Then we'd both say, "And goodnight for NBC News." Then we'd sometimes chat through the night, giggling, conspiring, arguing, tugging, pulling, and swapping secrets until our older brother Michael, occupying the single bed across from us, told us to shut up or he'd kick the crap out of us.

Occasionally our eldest brother, Brian, would make Greg and me lace up the boxing gloves in the garage and fight for the pleasure of kin and neighbor, which we welcomed with gusto. We roughly shared the same physical stature and fiery temperament, though Greg's fuse was slightly shorter than mine. He'd knock me down; I'd knock him down. Then we'd have tea, or more likely, a root beer.

All the Hannon boys at one time or another had afternoon paper routes, but Greg and I often helped each other out, finishing our routes together and then retiring to Sil's Restaurant on Foothill Boulevard for a pre-dinner repast of cheeseburgers and milkshakes or to Mr. Donut's, where we washed down day-old maple bars with Cokes, or to the Castro Village Lanes, where we bowled ten frames and feasted on grilled cheese sandwiches from the bowling alley restaurant. Half of our late night conversations in those years must have been brainstorming sessions during which we feverishly concocted plausible explanations for the absence of any profit from our respective paper routes at month's end, when our mother always demanded an accounting.

Greg and I shared everything: T-shirts and late-night television shows; coughs and colds and tooth brushes; a penchant for cussing under our breaths and for sneaking cigarettes from our mom's purse and puffing on them while riding our bikes in downtown Hayward. We served mass together as altar boys; Father McGovern asked for us constantly for funerals because we had both mastered the prayerfully sober look that the Irish have perfected over the centuries. And, I suppose, because we never dipped into the sacramental wine. Years later, when we were in our early teens, I think Greg and I even shared the same girlfriend, unbeknownst to either of us until a Sadie Hawkins dance at our high school exposed our beloved's duplicity.

The filial love my brother and I shared was unspoken; we had neither the maturity nor the inclination to put into words the bond of brotherhood we had forged. It was sufficient simply to put in the time and wile away the hours together and leave it up to others to draw their own conclusions. A phone call does not end now without Greg and I saying "I love you," but back then he was the brother with whom I slept. I couldn't have imagined my life without him.

Thus, what transpired one summer day long ago becomes all the more tragic, horrifying, and sadly unforgettable.

✤ ✤ ✤ ✤ ✤ ✤ ✤

When the invitation arrived that morning, when it slipped through the mail slot and landed on the worn, green carpet of our living room, my heart skipped a beat. Bob Gerstenberger, whom everyone affectionately referred to as "Boober" was having a birthday party the next weekend. Everyone my age knew about it. The Gerstenbergers were the closest thing to landed gentry in our working class neighborhood. The father was a dentist, so all of his five children had beautiful, straight, white teeth. Their front and back yards were meticulously landscaped, impeccably manicured, and though they sat on a lot no bigger than ours, it had the feel of a country estate. There were many things that the

Gerstenbergers had that the rest of Arcadian Drive pined for: a gas-powered lawn mower, a brand new 1965 station wagon whose rear hatch opened up from the side, an RCA stereo console with an eight-track tape component. When they secured the services of a full-time maid, well, we knew when to surrender. This was one Jones family none of us would ever be able to keep up with.

My family, on the other hand, most closely resembled peasants, even though our father was a lawyer and a highly respected one at that. Mom and Dad had brought ten of their own into the world, insuring that the versatile and inexpensive potato would grace the dinner table most every night. Our backyard was never expected to withstand the punishment we Hannon kids meted out to it on a regular basis. Graced with apricot, plum, peach, tangerine, lemon, and grapefruit trees, in most of our neighbors' eyes it had become a kind of paradise lost, complete with tree houses held together by a few rusty nails, mesh-wired coops with squawking chickens, a pitching mound, a lawn (only if you defined "lawn" in the broadest possible way), a clothesline twirling in the wind with the help of eight different sizes of underwear acting as sails, an elaborate archeological dig that unearthed nothing more than the remains of a guinea pig buried five summers before. Our garage was where we played roller derby and fought, bare-knuckled or otherwise. Most doors in our house had holes kicked into them, always by accident, we would tell Mom and Dad. We had no maid.

In fact, I remember one time as a youngster being at home by myself. Mom had to run a quick errand to the market, and though she told me not to even think about leaving the house, I did. It was noontime, which meant I had to have my lunch. And since Mom wasn't there, I walked down to the Gerstenbergers and knocked on their door. When the maid answered I told her my mother wasn't home and I was hungry. If she didn't mind, would she make me a peanut butter and jelly sandwich? She sent me home empty and told me to wait for my mother. We were all Philistines, and even the Gerstenberger's maid knew it.

So to get an invitation to Boober's birthday party was something pretty special. It was a chance to mingle with the rich, rub elbows with the country club elite, laugh and share vacation stories with the upper crust. "The Matterhorn? Why yes, I have been to the Matterhorn. I think it's the coolest ride in Disneyland. Oh, you mean the one in Switzerland?" I had it all planned out well beforehand: what I was going to wear; the gift Mom was going to buy for me to give to Boober; how this called for an extra dab of Dippity Doo and clean underwear. This was the big leagues, my chance to scale the wall that separated our two worlds and bask in the glory emanating from those who paid others to mow their lawns and cook their meals.

I arrived at the Gerstenbergers that morning as if it were the first day of the rest of my life. My younger sisters Margaret and Julie were held back as I left the house, which made me feel even more special. Their faces, pressed against the living room window, betrayed a mixture of envy and awe. Someone had to lift our family out of its lowly state, and I had been chosen. Six or seven kids were already waiting in the Gerstenberger's station wagon, so when I arrived I was sent to the back with a couple others, which was fine with me. We were on our way to the park for a party, and as I sat in the back seat I was overcome with a sense that *this* is what heaven must be like. Lost in paradise, I didn't realize that my brother Greg had arrived on his Schwinn and was standing by the car peering in, presumably to get my attention.

The next thing I remember hearing were words, ugly words, words that were meant to inflict immediate pain. A couple of my friends were yelling at my brother to get the heck away from the car, that he wasn't invited and should go home. I had never heard anyone my age cuss that loud before, and it startled me.

What startled me even more was the delayed reaction that registered on my brother's face. At first he thought my new, rich friends were kidding, and so he flashed an innocent smile. When the assault continued, it began to dawn on him that they were being mean, junkyard dog mean; snarling, vicious mean. As the blood began to slowly drain from Greg's face and collect in his ears, he looked at me as if to say, "What are *you* going to do about this?" My eyes met his and said clearly, silently, to my brother: "Go home; you're ruining everything." And then I turned away.

Acting as if he could read my mind, Greg got back on his bike and made his way up the street to our house. I saw him climb down off his bike, throw it against the side of the house, and run inside. He was sobbing.

The day continued as scheduled. We went to the park and had a party. We played games. But that whole afternoon all I really wanted to do was find a secluded corner somewhere and throw up.

Looking back I could count myself among those whom St. James criticized in his letter. "Come now, you rich," he wrote, "your wealth has rotted away." What riches I may have gained that afternoon had rotted, my fine clothes had grown moth eaten, the gold and silver I thought I had acquired corroded and stood as testimony against me. I was five, maybe six years old and had made a childish mistake. God had given me a voice to defend my brother and I hadn't used it. Afraid of losing the treasure I thought I had gained, I remained silent in the face of a grave injustice, blind to the irony that would haunt me for years: I already had a greater treasure in my brother and had turned my back on him.

As hard as it is to forgive others the wrongs they have done, sometimes it is even harder to forgive ourselves for the hurts we cause.

❀❀❀❀❀❀❀

A number of years ago, Greg and I were in a reminiscing mood, and I brought up the events of that summer morning. The memory was living and breathing in me still, and I was sobered by the chord of sadness it still struck in my heart. Then I discovered Greg had no memory whatsoever of that day! He rather enjoyed my recounting of it, though, in part because he sensed my residual guilt, and he was gratified that a betrayal so tattered and torn by the passage of time could still hold sway over my soul.

As hard as it is to forgive others the wrongs they have done, some-times it is even harder to forgive ourselves for the hurts we cause. When Thoreau observed that "most men lead lives of quiet desperation and go to the grave with the song still in them," I think he was mostly referring to those haunting memories of personal failures that many of us can't seem to let go of, either because we believe (wrongly) that they are un-forgivable or because they become so much part of the landscape of our lives we fear we would forever be lost should we leave them behind.

Somewhere along the way, I found the courage to forgive myself for a childish sin committed a long time ago. It had teeth, that sin of my youth, but now I know there is something greater, something that has a stronger grip on my life. It is love: the love between brothers, the love that finds its greatest expression in mercy.

Writing Straight with Crooked Lines

A few years ago I was on the "El" (the elevated train) in Chicago making my way down to the Loop. I love taking the Skokie Swift and the Red Line downtown. Gazing out the window as the train snakes through the tall grass of Chicago, past alleys and backyards, past old brick buildings with faded advertisements and broken windows, past busy crossroads of commerce and community, from my moving perch I always get the sense that I'm taking in the real Chicago, all grace and grit, a city of poetry and pawn shops as much as parks and politics.

It was a spectacular early spring afternoon. A thunderstorm had just lumbered through, leaving in its wake asphalt and concrete glittering in the wet sunlight. It was as if the city was waking up from a deep sleep and shaking off the last remaining shadow of night. The great Chicago poet Carl Sandburg once wrote, "Come and show me another city with lifted head singing so proud to be alive and coarse and strong and cunning." You could feel the pulse of the city quickening that afternoon; you could hear a city clearing its voice, getting ready to belt a tune.

As we pulled into the Addison Street station (right next to Wrigley Field), I observed a young man and woman in their early twenties on the platform engaged in what appeared to be a heated conversation. They looked the professional type: he in a tailored suit and silk tie and oxford wingtips pleading with her of manicured fingernails and subtle makeup and high heels. He was gripping the woman's arm with one hand while using his other to plead. You got the sense that this was the tail end of an argument that had begun a long time ago. Her face was lost in long dark hair, and the man kept ducking down trying to meet her eyes with his, desperately grasping at the waning moments of a broken relationship. She would have none of it, though, and when the doors to the train opened she shook off his grip and made her way onto the train, leaving him standing alone on the station platform.

The whole encounter took less than a minute and seemed oddly out of place, occurring at a time when it felt as if the whole world was being reborn. The man stood there like a statue as the train pulled out of the station. An expression of deep sadness crept upon his face. It was no doubt dawning on him that in a city of millions he was now utterly and completely alone. For a second, my eyes caught the young man's left hand. I noticed he was wearing a wedding ring. I quickly glanced over to the woman who was walking away from me and toward an empty seat by the far door. Her wedding finger was graced with a band as well.

As the train lurched along, I thought about the young man, wondering what he would do next. Maybe he staggered to the nearest watering hole, climbed onto a barstool, loosened his tie, and directed the barkeep to keep them coming. Maybe he went back to work and spent the rest of the afternoon sitting at his desk, staring into the void. Maybe he went to a church and sat in a pew and called upon God to do something—anything—to make the pain go away. Wherever he ended up, I knew he would be lost—at least for a while—with his heart unanchored, drifting in fog and feeling very much alone.

When the train pulled into my station, I made my way to the exit. Sitting right in front of me was the woman. She looked like she had been punched in the stomach, pale and unpoised, teetering on the edge of some dark abyss. I wouldn't be surprised if she were still riding that train, paralyzed by ineffable pain.

This brief encounter is the stuff of country and western songs: lost loves, broken hearts, and long, lonely journeys. The moment we open our hearts to the possibility of love, we open ourselves to the possibility of pain and hurt as well. There is no escaping it. We are born with an amazing capacity to love, and therefore we have the real possibility of losing everything. We willingly hand over our hearts to another and emphatically still the voice deep within that warns us of betrayal and rejection. Maybe it is one of the residues of original sin that most of us carry with us—at the very least—a hint of fear that the one who loves us now might turn a cold shoulder one day, that the lips we kiss now will one day part and whisper goodbye.

Yet despite the risks and dangers, we continue to seek out others to forge new friendships and open our hearts to the possibility of love. For even though jukeboxes in dusty taverns are filled with songs of lost love and broken hearts, we continue to dance to the beat, to hope, to dream.

❁ ❁ ❁ ❁ ❁ ❁ ❁

Not long ago, two parishioners at Sacred Heart in Colorado Springs, Roger and Sandy Strempke, celebrated their twenty-fifth anniversary. They invited me to preside at their anniversary mass on a Saturday afternoon that was attended by their four children and a hundred of their friends. Roger and Sandy are Catholic. He is a Knight of Columbus; she teaches CCD to third graders. They go to mass every Sunday, sitting in their favorite pew, fourth one down on the right. They also work with engaged couples in the parish marriage preparation program and are Eucharistic ministers.

It was wonderful witnessing how they saw their wedding vows through the lens of a community that stakes its entire existence on the values of unity and peace, the mother's milk of married life. With twenty-five years of marriage and family life under their belts, the Strempkes stood up and said in so many words, "Let's do this for another twenty-five!"

Roger stood facing his wife and, holding the words of his vows in his trembling hands, he reaffirmed his love for Sandy, promising to be true to her for the rest of his life. His words were of heartfelt thanksgiving, echoing the refrain of most husbands through the ages: I am the luckiest man in the world to have a woman like you by my side. Glistening eyes and quivering lips made this a transfiguring moment. Roger was young again; a quarter century was dissolved happily by bliss. His bride was still by his side.

Then Sandy began to speak. Her prefatory comments, I do not remember. But they led to her main testimonial to the power of married life: "Roger, you are my best friend and my worst enemy…." The rest of what she said merely polished the gold of that declaration, making it brilliant and stunning. "You are my best friend and my worst enemy." At first blush it seems like an alarming statement. But when you give it a second hearing, it testifies to a kind of resiliency that finds its origin in the Divine. It is an honest appraisal of the best of marriages, because it so closely resembles our relationship with God.

The question that Christian marriage attempts to answer is this: Are we willing to trust in the power of love to heal all things? No one chooses to be married in the Church because they think it is the easiest choice among life's many options. A man and woman choose to be Christian spouses and Christian parents because it will demand everything from them and because they believe that the imperfect love they bring to each other can and will be transforming. They might be best friends at some times and worst enemies at other times, but they are willing to trust and believe that God writes most magnificently straight with incredibly crooked lines.

A man and woman choose to be Christian spouses and Christian parents because they believe that the imperfect love they bring to each other can and will be transforming.

In Paul's first letter to the Corinthians, he spoke of such love, and that passage may very well be the most often read scripture at Christian weddings. "Love does not insist on its own way," Paul wrote. "It does not rejoice over wrongdoings, but rejoices in the truth. It bears all things, believes all things, hopes all things, endures all things."

"Love," Paul triumphantly concluded, "never ends."

❖ ❖ ❖ ❖ ❖ ❖ ❖

There was in Chicago a young man and woman who may very well still be alone somewhere, licking the wounds of their broken hearts. I hope not. I hope that they got back together. I hope they came to see what Roger and Sandy have come to marvel at after twenty-five years of marriage: Sometimes the one you love will drive you absolutely crazy. Mostly I hope that Chicago couple has come to see that through it all

God does keep His promises and that, though we may love imperfectly, such love will never end.

Coming Back Home

I will get up and go to my father,
and I will say to him,
"Father, I have sinned against heaven and before you.
I am no longer worthy to be called your son;
treat me like one of your hired hands."
So he set off and went to his father.
But while he was still far off,
his father saw him
and was filled with compassion;
he ran and put his arms around him
and kissed him.

Luke 15

Dorothy Day once wrote, "All my life I have been haunted by God." The older I get the more I think I understand what she meant. I burrow into the heart of that young man in the parable of the Prodigal Son and try to feel what he feels, because his story is so much like my own that it's almost frightening. I see what he sees: my father running out to embrace me; his arms around my cold and shivering body; his kiss on my cheek. I hear the sobbing words of love whispered in my ear, and I'm left speechless, helpless, haunted. This father of mine will not let me go. His tears bathe me in mercy. I've done terrible things, shameful things; things that I hope never see the light of day. And then, there he is, this father of mine, not a hint of hurt or anger or disappointment on his face. He must be absolutely mad. All my life I, too, have been haunted by God.

❖ ❖ ❖ ❖ ❖ ❖ ❖

One time, I was talking with a woman I've gotten to know here in Colorado Springs. Her son had recently bought the watering hole down the street from the church called "Meadow Muffins," and she was proud as a peacock. Back in my novitiate days, I told her, my novice brothers and I brought the bust of our founder Blessed Basil Moreau down the mountain with us one evening to Meadow Muffins. We had dressed him in a Cleveland Indian's jacket and had him sitting with us at the bar, a cigarette taped to his mouth. (Now *that* is religious life.)

Never walk away from someone who is dying; they have so much to teach us about living.

After a while, however, the conversation with this woman turned a bit more serious. Eileen is fifty-nine years old. Her husband died when he was forty-five and she was only thirty-six. In the last days of his life, she says, they did a lot of cuddling on the couch. As she held him and he held her, she kept on thinking to herself, "How am I ever going to live without him?" And at one point before he died, Eileen's husband told her, "Honey, remember two things: I will always love you and, more importantly, God's grace will always be sufficient." Eileen looked up at me and then said the most remarkable thing. She said, "I tell people: Never walk away from someone who is dying; they have so much to teach us about living."

❖ ❖ ❖ ❖ ❖ ❖ ❖

I once had a conversation with a sixteen-year-old girl on the bench outside the parish center in Colorado Springs. Her grandmother dropped her off at the church and told her not to come home until she had talked to a priest. At one point in the conversation, I asked Sonia what she was most afraid of, because after a half hour of conversation it had become apparent to me that it had to be fear of something that was holding her back. She was a girl who didn't seem to be afraid of anything. She was tough-skinned and tattooed and carried a taunting air about her, her hands in their default fisted position. Her brother was in jail; her dad was in prison, and she hadn't seen her mother in ten years. Her grandmother, the only person she trusts in the whole world, has high blood pressure and diabetes and a bad heart. (Judging by the way the grandmother peeled out of the parking lot, she must have a checkered driving history as well!)

Sonia looked right at me with eyes traced thick with eye liner and said, "What am I most afraid of, Father? I'll tell you what I'm most afraid of. I'm afraid that God won't ever forgive me for some of the things I've done." I thought Sonia might have said going to jail or getting pregnant or getting knifed, but she said she was most afraid that God was not merciful enough. Where did she get such an idea? Where do any of us get such an idea?

Suddenly, I remembered the day forty-three years ago, when I was four and half years old. I had taken my brother's B-B gun and it accidentally went off in the kitchen and shattered the statue of the Blessed Virgin Mary that hung over the sink. I remember hearing my mother shriek as I high-tailed it out of the house. I made my way up the hill and into the patch of thick woods that bordered our neighborhood.

There I sat on a rock, trying to figure out how I was ever going to make it back home again. I could not, despite the consistently unconditional love of my parents, imagine a way. How could my mother ever forgive me? It would be years later before I could begin to put that experience of separation into words, but that day I began my lifelong spiritual journey.

Seeing that little boy propped on a big rock all alone, longing for the necessary strength to reverse the orbit of the earth and to go back to that time before the Fall, before Mary's porcelain head was shot off by a wayward B-B, and knowing that wishing for it doesn't make it so, I understood what Sonia was going through.

"I'm afraid that God won't ever forgive me for some of the things I've done," she said. These are words that mark the miles of separation we feel in the marrow of our bones, words that say essentially, "Can I ever go back home again?" The Christian spiritual journey, the one that traces the steps of Jesus as he made his way to the hill of Calvary, is one that has a healthy appreciation for the effect of sin. It is a journey that reminds us, sometimes daily, that our hearts are always restless for home. And so, we can understand and readily appreciate what Dorothy Day also said: "We have all known the long loneliness, and we have learned that the only solution is love and that love comes with community." She was right. This "long loneliness" of which Dorothy Day spoke is the hidden subtext of the parable of the Prodigal Son, and it is the subtext of our story too: yours, mine, Sonia's.

❧ ❧ ❧ ❧ ❧ ❧

Remember the movie *Moonstruck*? There's a great scene at the airport when Loretta (the Cher character) has said goodbye to her fiancé, who is flying back to Palermo, Italy, to be at his mother's deathbed. Standing next to the window, looking out on the runways, is an old, black-shawled Sicilian woman.

In the background we see the accordion-like ramp that was connected to the departing aircraft slowly fold up. Loretta walks up beside the old woman and looks out the window at the plane.

The old woman notices Loretta and asks, "Do you have someone on that plane?"

"Yeah," Loretta answers, and she smiles. "My fiancé."

"I have put a curse on that plane," says the old woman. "My sister is on that plane. I have put a curse on that plane that it should explode. Burn on fire and fall into the sea. Fifty years ago she stole a man from me. Today she told me that she didn't even love him. She took him to feel strong with me. Now she goes back to Sicily. I have cursed her that the green Atlantic water should swallow her up."

"I don't believe in curses," says Loretta.

"Neither do I," says the old woman, and she smiles.

❧ ❧ ❧ ❧ ❧ ❧

"There was man who had two sons." So begins the greatest story in the Gospels, the gospel within the Gospels, someone once called it. It is a story of mercy, of a father who is completely, madly in love with us. It is a story of how sin and grace went at it, and how sin was pinned to the mat.

It is a story about leaving home, of a journey to a distant land, of one son who wondered if you can ever really go home again, of another son who can't forgive and therefore gets left out of the party. Really, it is our story, yours and mine, and Sonia's.

FOUR

A View from the Mountaintop
Seeing What God Sees

For it was you who formed my inward parts;
you knit me together in my mother's womb.
I praise you,
for I am fearfully and wonderfully made.
Wonderful are your works;
that I know very well.
My frame was not hidden from you,
when I was being made in secret,
intricately woven in the depths of the earth.
Your eyes beheld my unformed substance.
In your book were written
all the days that were formed for me,
when none of them as yet existed.
How weighty to me are your thoughts, O God!
How vast is the sum of them!
I try to count them—
they are more than the sand.

Psalm 139

The Rooftop of the World

Willi Unsoeld, the American climber who was part of the first American expedition to the summit of Mt. Everest in 1963, said later, "You've climbed the highest mountain in the world. What's left? It's all downhill from there. You've got to set your sights on something higher than Everest." For him, climbing Mt. Everest was a means to an end. He wrote later, "You go to nature for an experience of the sacred... to re-establish your contact with the core of things, where it's really at, in order to enable you to come back to the world of people and operate more effectively." Unsoeld suggests something rather extraordinary: Exhilarating and compelling as the ascent to the top of a mountain may be, the power and grace of the climb is in the descent, coming back to the world of people and to the core of things.

Sometimes when the spirit beckons you to go deeper inside—to the core of things—the journey you take to get there means you will breathe rarified air. Sometimes the quickest way to the deepest part of the human heart is by way of a mountain. Both journeys require guts and brawn and a bit of lunacy. But at the end of the journey, you get to see what God sees. It's worth the effort.

❖ ❖ ❖ ❖ ❖ ❖ ❖

In September of 1982, my housemates Maggie, Beth, M. J., Ted, and I climbed Pikes Peak, the glacier-sculpted piece of pink granite—all 14,115 feet of her—that graces the southern front range of the Colorado Rocky Mountains. We were all in our early twenties, volunteers signed up to spend a year of service in Colorado Springs, living an intentionally simple life centered on Christian community, work, and prayer. None of us had climbed a mountain before, but as we arrived at the Trailhead in Manitou Springs (elevation: 6,600 feet) at dawn, the sky was crystal clear and the trail to Barr Camp (elevation: 10,400 feet) was bedded with well-trampled early autumn leaves. Most importantly, other hikers abounded.

An elderly couple skipped past us with all deliberate speed, unintention-ally throwing down the gauntlet. Hell, I thought, if *they* can do it, *we* certainly can!

As we began our ascent, I was drawn back into time, long before Zebulon Pike made his historic climb to the top (which, incidentally, he never reached; a blizzard drove him back down), and I saw the ghosts of Ute Indians emerging from their tree-barked wickiups early in the morning, surrounded by ponderosa pine and blue spruce, feeding their horses, rousing the children, anticipating the long trek across the plains and the buffalo hunt that awaited. It was a bit nippy, so I zipped up my windbreaker and stuck my hands deeper into my pockets. The old couple I had seen earlier had long disappeared into the forest, leaving in their wake a wisp of anticipation and urgency.

Barr Trail snakes up the eastern slope of Pikes Peak. It begins at Manitou Mountain and concludes at the summit, eight miles away. Fred Barr, a thirty-eight-year-old mountain stage coach driver, single-hand-edly surveyed and meticulously built the trail over three summers, fin-ishing up on Christmas Eve, 1918. Ellen O'Connor, a reporter for the local paper, the *Gazette-Telegraph*, made this observation a few years later: "No small task this blazing of trails thru rocks, forest thickets and flood-washed ravines of the mountain slope! It means work, days and weeks of hard labor after the mind has laid out the path, the eye visioned its every steep rise. It means hours in the mountains, close to the heart of nature, a sort of friendly battle with nature until at last all her obstacles are removed and a path creeps upward."

We arrived at Barr Camp, a half-way point of campsites and pine wood cabins Fred Barr built in the 1920s for climbers and burro teams, and I was a bit winded. But the hike had thus far been spectacular, as we were treated to stunning vistas of rolling alpine terrain with aspen forests and meadows of wild flowers. The fickle Pikes Peak weather was chang-ing. Dark clouds had rolled in and it had begun to drizzle. My house-mates and I filled up our water bottles and ate the rest of our trail mix.

An hour later, somewhere up around 11,500 feet, past the tree line where the last of the ancient dwarf trees have dwindled away and the forest abruptly turns into tundra meadows, it began to thunder and light-ning. Rain was coming down at us sideways. We stumbled beneath a rocky overhang and sought shelter there along with a half dozen other hikers. I asked the group where they were from and they told me they were visiting from Oregon. What town? I asked, hoping I could whittle them down to Portland, a place I knew well. When they said they were from Salem, I half-jokingly asked if they knew my friend Mike Jaeger who was from there, insinuating a kind of intimacy arising from our shared experience in the global village. (How many times had someone asked *me*—having uncovered my Californian roots—if I knew so and so from Torrance or Laguna Beach or Pasadena? "Gee, I'm sorry," I'd say, "I don't know her. I'm actually from *northern* California." They always looked disappointed by my response.)

But, of course, one of them knew Mike Jaeger. He had dated the friend of his older brother or something like that. I think this guy worked for Salem's Chamber of Commerce because he wouldn't stop talking about all the great things about his hometown. I was initially touched by his gushy affection for the place, but when he began his lecture on traffic patterns in the downtown business district, I figured it was time to head out; rain, sleet, snow, or hail be damned.

Rain did turn to sleet and then to snow. I was in a pair of Levi's, a T-shirt and windbreaker, and my trusty Converse high-tops, and *I* was the overdressed one among our group. Later, after we had reached the summit, we were told that when it starts to snow the sane climber *descends* the mountain. I, however, had done the quick math and come to the conclusion that we were much closer to the summit than we were to the Trailhead, so I voted to continue climbing.

By the time we arrived at the "Sixteen Golden Stairs," a series of short, steep switch-backs in the final one-half mile to the summit, we were facing white-out conditions. We were reduced to slow, heavy steps, each one deliberate, purposeful. At 14,000 feet your oxygen is reduced to around sixty percent of normal, so breathing becomes labored and tortu-ous. We were literally sucking air. Beth was probably in the worst state; looking back, she most certainly was suffering from mild hypothermia.

We made it to the top of Pikes Peak that early afternoon and were greeted by winds in excess of eighty miles per hour and icy snow drifts and the gawky faces of more seasoned climbers in the warm lodge who pitied us the way one might pity little children who have not yet gained the requisite common sense that staves off premature death. We used the pay phone there in the café to call Brother Kenny Allen from the Holy Cross novitiate to drive up and retrieve us. Not a loquacious man to begin with, Brother Ken let us know as gently as he could—which was not very—that we were lucky to be alive. None of us was looking forward to the drive home with him, a man who volunteered regularly to go on winter ski rescue patrols among the hidden crevices of the Rockies. The tone of his voice on the phone told us he wasn't kidding: We were indeed lucky to be alive. Later that evening we learned that two hikers caught in that very storm were missing. They were never found.

✿ ✿ ✿ ✿ ✿ ✿ ✿

Why does anyone climb a mountain? When asked why he was climbing Mt. Everest, the English climber George Mallory replied tersely, "Because it is there." But by the time he was asked that question, he had already attempted to reach the top of the world twice, and his third and last attempt probably ended in failure as well. His body wasn't found for seventy-five years, and it was unclear whether he had been on his way up or on his way down.

Why would anyone want to climb over 29,000 feet into thin cobalt air? You have to be a little crazy. Tibetans refer to Mt. Everest as "Chomolungma" ("goddess mother of the world"). After months and months of preparation, this is what you can anticipate if you try to climb her: avalanches, deep crevasses, ferocious winds up to 125 mph, sudden storms, temperatures of 40°F below zero, and oxygen deprivation. In the "death zone"—above 25,000 feet—the air holds only a third as much oxygen as at sea level, heightening the chances of hypothermia, frostbite, high-altitude pulmonary edema (when the lungs fatally fill with fluid), and high-altitude cerebral edema (when the oxygen-starved brain swells up). Even when breathing bottled oxygen, climbers experience extreme fatigue, impaired judgment and coordination, headaches, nausea, double vision, and sometimes hallucinations.

And yet Stacy Allison, the first American woman to reach the summit of Everest described it this way: "The end of the ridge and the end of the world...then nothing but that clear, empty air. There was nowhere else to climb. I was standing on the top of the world." She was surveying the world from its top; only commercial jets flying a few thousand feet higher could see what she saw. Risking life and limb, knowing that the journey is more purgatory than paradise, resigned to a task that is Herculean and hellish and nearly hopeless (the deepest part of Dante's hell was ice, of course), many among our species still rest their eyes upon a distant, magnificent summit and say, "I will conquer you."

For it is really not so much getting to the top that matters most. It is the attempt, the willingness to sacrifice and suffer, the patient and oftentimes agonizing endurance that allows us, in a sense, to see what God sees.

I used to think it was rather romantic to climb to the top of a mountain and survey in one wide sweep of the gaze all that the human eye can capture. Now I think it is mostly lunacy. But it is also holiness. For it is really not so much getting to the top that matters most. It is the attempt, the willingness to sacrifice and suffer, the patient and oftentimes agonizing endurance that allows us, in a sense, to see what God sees. We are looking to find, as Willi Unsoeld hoped, something in ourselves that will make a difference after the descent.

In the Dark

If I should pass the tomb of Jonah
I would stop there and sit for awhile,
Because I was swallowed one time deep in the dark
And came out alive after all.

Carl Sandburg

The first thing you need to know about me for the purpose of this story is that I never wanted to move to the Midwest.

Seven weeks into my first year at Notre Dame High School in Niles, a suburb of Chicago, I'm sitting at a table on an unusually cold October evening talking with the mother of one of my students, and she is asking me where I came from. When I tell her California, she looks at me quizzically—you know, with the horrified gawk usually reserved for sideshow exhibits in traveling carnivals. "Why in God's name would you want to move from California to Chicago?" she asks in all sincerity.

Why, indeed. But I tell her what I want to believe: I love a new challenge; I heard Chicago is a great town; I wanted to get back into teaching.

I go on and on, but the honest-to-God truth is that it was the vow of obedience—the quiet sibling of those sacred vows members of religious communities make—that got me here. It was obedience and obedience alone. As I said, the first thing you need to know about me for the purpose of this story is that I never wanted to move to the Midwest.

❖ ❖ ❖ ❖ ❖ ❖ ❖

My students—all male—think celibacy must be the toughest vow to embrace, and given their hormonal state I don't blame them for thinking that. Or sometimes they figure it must be the vow of poverty, given their own lifestyles and aspirations. ("How do you live on only a hundred and fifty bucks a month, Father?") But I promise you that it is really and truly the vow of obedience that has kept me up nights, sweating and rethinking the trajectory of my life and making me more humble than I ever wanted to be.

I suspect I am not unlike most everyone else in this regard, especially spouses and parents. Stitched into married life is a kind of obedience that requires great sacrifices, too. Both theologically and practically speaking, obedience means our lives are never truly our own. Parents and spouses live that truth out every day, and so do men and women who take religious vows.

So it happened that five years ago I packed all of my belongings into cardboard boxes and made the trek from San Francisco to Chicago. I was beginning a new ministry in a new town with a group of Holy Cross priests I did not know. I was thirty-nine years old—a novice middle-ager living 2,000 miles away from my nearest kin. I told my family and friends that this would be a three-year gig and that with my provincial superior's blessing, and God willing, I would return like the prodigal son, to bask once again in the warmth of familial love and west coast sun.

❖ ❖ ❖ ❖ ❖ ❖

The second thing you need to know about me is that I'm Irish, to the marrow of my bones. There is a strain of us called the "I'm-never-truly-happy-unless-I'm-sad" Irish. Depression runs in my family, and all of my brothers and sisters (and their spouses) agree it is because of the Celtic blood that courses through our veins. The Irish writer Edna O'Brien put it this way: "When anyone asks me about the Irish character, I say look at the trees. Maimed, stark and misshapen, but ferociously tenacious." We're the kind of Irishmen who are genuinely cheerful on the outside. We exhibit a spirit that betrays a gritty determination to endure, but on the inside, well, there sits the sad poet.

Now, our *particular* strand of Irish, namely, the Hannon clan, finds its greatest joy in pleasing others. Growing up, we were the ones you wanted to invite to your parties or enlist for some huge project. We were the best chemistry lab partners. We lived to make other people happy. The greatest sin any of us could commit was the sin of disappointing someone else. (Though we only occasionally practiced such generosity among our siblings, the rest of the world loved us Hannon kids.)

❖ ❖ ❖ ❖ ❖ ❖

These two dominant traits—the propensity toward melancholy and the desire to please—finally came home to roost for me seven weeks into my stint at Notre Dame High School.

I had moved because I was asked to, because I wanted to be an obedient son. But, unbeknownst to almost everyone at the school—my colleagues, students, and most of my Holy Cross confreres—I was being sucked deeper and deeper into an unfamiliar darkness, a darkness I began to fear would swallow me whole.

My depression was like waking up on a different planet. I distinctly remember walking one morning in early August along the breezeway that connects the school to the priests' residence with a growing feeling of apprehension and uncertainty that I had never before experienced. At first, I dismissed it as first-day jitters. After all, it had been nine years since I had taught full time. If I hadn't been nervous, I would have been worried! (How's that for Irish optimism?)

But somehow I knew that this was more than nervousness. Much the way one senses with the first scratch in the throat that it's more than a cold, I knew that I was dealing with something far more serious than stage fright. Yet the farthest point on my new horizon bore only the faintest hint of the brewing storm.

I walked into my first period class, British Literature with seniors, completely out of my element. I was standing before what appeared to be the entire offensive and defensive lines of the varsity football team, twenty-eight young men who carried themselves with a Chicago swagger and spoke with a kind of street-smart cockiness that had me pining immediately for those kind old ladies that kept me knee-deep in devotion and chocolate-chip cookies at the parish I had left behind.

I made it through the first day—barely—and collapsed in a chair in my bedroom that afternoon. I slept through dinner. It was the beginning of my first—but not my last—episode of major depression.

❖ ❖ ❖ ❖ ❖ ❖ ❖

My students were (and are) amazing human beings. After a few short weeks I got used to the all-male environment of Notre Dame. It is not unlike a tight-knit family, a fraternity of brothers. It amazes me still to witness the kind of fierce loyalty and pride such a learning environment engenders in the hearts of young men. In my first weeks in the teaching saddle, the Dons of Notre Dame (a Don is a Gentleman) coaxed the best out of me.

Beowulf, Blake, Shakespeare, and Shelly: I was determined to shape their minds and hearts with the tools of prose and verse. Knowing how much I loved literature and writing, they mostly went along, feigning disinterest but secretly hoping I would inspire them.

But even as I summoned my will and energy every morning to teach, I was beginning to die a little every day. The seeping sadness took over my sleep first. I began waking up in the middle of the night and lay there until together my alarm clock and I welcomed the dawn. It took every ounce of energy to get out of bed. I would sit through Morning Prayer with my Holy Cross community, and I found many of the psalms bemusing at best, cruel at worst. "Save me, O God," Psalm 69 begins, "for the waters have come up to my neck. I sink in deep mire, where there is no foothold.... I am weary with my crying." And Psalm 53 starts out, "O God, you are my God, I seek you, my soul thirsts for you; my flesh faints for you, as in a dry and weary land where there is no water."

Only later would I come to appreciate that the gnawing pain of anguish that I felt those mornings was prayer, and though it seemed as if God had turned a deaf ear to my constant pleas, in retrospect God was there with me, sharing my suffering, making it His own.

❀ ❀ ❀ ❀ ❀ ❀

By the time I arrived in my classroom each morning, I was usually fine. I thoroughly enjoyed the respite that my workload provided me: teaching, counseling, moderating a club. I actually did a phenomenal job hiding the truth; and I'm glad I did. My students needed me to be at my best. Whatever personal trials I was enduring were properly left at the classroom door.

I recall later that semester one of my seniors asking me with well-honed skepticism how it was possible for me to be so happy and positive all the time. Not telling him the truth—that even getting dressed in the morning was a painful decision—brought me secret satisfaction as well. Inside, I was like the poet's Irish tree: "maimed, stark and misshapen." But outside I was still able to be "ferociously tenacious."

My depression came down to a lack of trust. I was having a very difficult time accepting the possibility that it was God's will for me to be in Illinois, teaching English to a bunch of boys I didn't know. It made absolutely no sense that I should be exiled so far away from family and friends, from anything that was familiar to me. I was deeply lonely, and that loneliness drew me into a defensive, isolating crouch. I spent most of my free time by myself.

Weekends were the worst, for the one thing that kept me tethered to any semblance of stability was my academic routine. Many a weekend night I spent on the phone with a trusted friend or a brother or a sister; and mostly I cried. It wasn't supposed to be this hard! I had already buried my mother and father and the one grandparent I had ever really known. I knew what it was like to love and lose. And though I had long accepted the fact that life could be cruel and bitter at times, it seemed ludicrous to have to walk that lonely road severed from my loved ones, all because I had made a promise to obey my religious superiors. The pain seemed so banal and tedious.

We must discern first

our heart's deepest desire,

and done that,

we will discover

what God's deepest desire

is for us as well.

People ask me how we are to discern God's will for us. I tell them that we must discern first *our* heart's deepest desire, and done that, we will discover what God's deepest desire is for us as well.

At first I thought my deepest desire was to return home and go to as many Oakland A's games as possible. I thought my heart's deepest desire was to take a bottle of California Cabernet to Baker Beach at dusk and toast the sunset as it slipped behind the placid Pacific, casting the Golden Gate Bridge in a light both hieratic and profound. I thought my heart's deepest desire was to "get the hell out of Dodge." Every night I prayed to God to instruct my heart in His ways, to help me make sense of my suffering. Every morning I prayed—actually demanded—that God let me know, in a timely manner, what I was supposed to do. And every night and every morning the only words I heard from God in my heart were two: "Trust me." And those two words depressed me to the bottom of my soul.

I began to lose weight. When I went home for a quick visit over Thanksgiving weekend, my family thought I had cancer. I finally began to let my brothers in community know that I was in a desperate struggle to survive. Such is the insidious nature of depression that it makes us believe things that simply aren't true. I thought I was a complete flop in and out of the classroom. I looked at myself in the mirror and observed a failure—a weak, frightened, pathetic creature—despite every assurance from others to the contrary. I simply did not believe them.

Nonetheless, I held on. I had too much in the game now to fold. I was going to see my hand through. "Trust me," was all God would say to me in those dark days. It was a gamble, but I hadn't much else to lose.

❄ ❄ ❄ ❄ ❄ ❄

That December, right near the end of the first semester, I had met with a mother of one of my seniors. She had asked to see me because she was concerned about her son's academic performance. The boy was not a particularly disciplined student, and he was struggling to maintain a D in my course. I assumed he wasn't faring much better in his other classes.

The mother was not much older than I. She was a single mom, working two jobs so her son might attend a Catholic high school. At one point in our conversation, after assuring her that I would continue to work with her son so he would get a passing grade, I began to tell her of the potential I saw in his writing. Sure, he was a bit sloppy and inconsistent in his prose, I said, but he had a bit of the poet in him. I showed her some of his writing and pointed out where I saw real promise. With enough hard work and encouragement, I told her, I thought he could be a promising writer.

And then I thanked her. I told her that poets are almost always born first in the hearts of their mothers and that it is usually the case that writers are nurtured by the encouragement of the ones who love them. In her son's case, it was she who needed to be thanked for tending to a young mind and heart in its most formative period. I thanked her for being a great mom.

Suddenly, she began to cry. I knew immediately they were tears of both joy and sadness.

I realized she was hearing—maybe for the first time in a long time—that she was not a failure, that she really was doing an amazing job raising a son all on her own. I saw sadness because maybe she had come perilously close to surrendering to the darkness of despair.

"Father Pat," she said, "there's something you need to know, something none of John's classmate's know. Tomorrow," she continued, "John will be celebrating his first year of sobriety. He is a recovering heroin addict."

She proceeded to tell me of her son's middle-school years when he had first experimented with marijuana and then alcohol, and then how in the eighth grade he had gotten hooked on heroin. She told me of his slow progress back to health and how grateful he was to be at Notre Dame because it placed a healthy distance between him and those with whom he associated during his drinking and drugging days. She told me how he was so looking forward to the next day, when he would celebrate his "first birthday."

By the end of our conversation we both were in tears, and afterward it began to dawn on me that maybe God had indeed answered my prayers. Perhaps I now knew why I had been asked to move to Chicago. Perhaps it was my heart's deepest desire to stay. In one brief encounter with the mother of one of my students, both of our suffering had been laid bare, and for both of us the suffering had become redemptive.

I remember that Thomas Merton often talked about the idea of redemptive suffering. For Christians, suffering of any sort becomes redemptive, he said, when we willingly hand it over to God, trusting in the healing power of the redeeming cross of His Son, Jesus Christ.

John's mother and I had walked alone for a long time up our separate mountains, our individual Calvary hills until—at that one graced moment in time—we began to walk together.

Those first months at Notre Dame were for me three long days in the tomb. I was asked by my superiors to come to Chicago—unbeknownst to them or to me—so that I might come to trust God more completely. I had to leave home and loved ones in order to see my familial and tribal predisposition for melancholy as a gift of sorts and not a burden.

At the end of Mark's gospel, when the three women arrive at the tomb of Jesus only to find that the huge stone covering the entrance had been rolled away, they saw a young man sitting on the right side, clothed in a white robe. "Do not be alarmed," the young man urged them. "You are looking for Jesus of Nazareth, who was crucified. He has been raised; he is not here."

Five years ago, I was swallowed by a deep darkness; and for a while I lay helpless in a tomb. And then one day, a young man, one who had spent the better part of a year putting on new garments of sobriety, garments that would heal the syringe marks on his body and make him new again, rolled the stone away for me. His name was John, and he was the angel who came to tell me that there was reason to trust, to hope, to hold on.

FIVE

The Winding River
Healing Mercy

Then he led me back along the bank of the river.
As I came back,
I saw on the bank of the river a great many trees
on the one side and on the other.
He said to me,
"This water flows toward the eastern region
and goes down into the Arabah;
and when it enters the sea,
the sea of stagnant waters,
the water will become fresh.
Wherever the river goes,
every living creature that swarms will live,
and there will be many fish,
once these waters reach there.
It will become fresh;
and everything will live where the river goes....
On the banks, on both sides of the river,
there will grow all kinds of trees for food.
Their leaves will not wither nor their fruit fail,
but they will bear fresh fruit each month,
because the water for them flows from the sanctuary.
Their fruit will be for food,
and their leaves for healing."

Ezekiel 47

River of Mercy

The river's formal name, the one given it by Spanish explorer Gabriel Moraga in 1802, is El Rio Nuestra Senora de la Merced, or "The River of Our Lady of Mercy." Apparently he and his companions came upon this river after a hot, dry, and dusty ride. Today we refer to it simply as the Merced River, River of Mercy. It tumbles over the Nevada and Vernal Falls and weaves its way through the southern edge of the granite valley of Yosemite before heading into the San Joaquin valley on its way to the Pacific Ocean. Parts of the river from April to July—flush and exuberant from the winter Sierra snow pack—provide a wild white-water ride, but by late summer she is reduced to a mere trickle.

The late spring I was there back in 1987, my tent pitched a stone's throw from its edge, the Merced was tranquil and quiet, its disposition not unlike that of a solitary child at play, happily lost in unselfconsciousness. I was with a Jesuit friend, Drew Christiansen—a much more able camper than I—who taught me all sorts of camping skills, not the least of which was how to pick out the right tree and branch over which we would sling our canvass bag of food at night, dangling from a rope out of the reach of a Black bear's paw and drooling jaw.

We hiked the canyons in the day and prayed and read and meditated under the sun; and at night we ate charcoal-tinted food and let a nip of wine pass our lips by the river's edge. And we prayed and celebrated mass and eventually retired to our thermal underwear and sleeping bags and to the vagaries of the valley's vernal night. My heart was drawn to the Merced, to its trickling song, somnolent in the starry early morning, playful at noon, seductive in the moonlight.

❀ ❀ ❀ ❀ ❀ ❀ ❀

Sitting by the bank of the Merced, I remembered how important rivers were to Jesus, how they must have fed his religious imagination. He probably crossed one in the arms of Mary when she and Joseph fled

Herod's jealous wrath to Egypt soon after Jesus was born. How Joseph must have loved to regale Jesus with the story of *that* journey before his bedtime, even knowing that it would have kept Jesus awake in wonder and excitement long into the night.

As quickly as he had jumped in,

something jumped out of him,

for he began to float,

light and feather-like,

as if the river had claimed that which

he wanted to leave behind.

Jesus grew up a few miles away from the Jordan River, the river Joshua crossed with his shackle-freed tribe on their way to the Promised Land; the river where the prophet Elisha healed the leper Naaman; the river where Jesus met up with his cousin John and allowed him to baptize him. In so doing, Jesus united himself completely to our humanity. We do not have a high priest, the writer of the Letter to the Hebrews wrote, who is not able to sympathize with our weakness. This was Jesus, and he was dunked in the Jordan River like a sinner and came out refreshed and ready to face the desert. He knew that the Jordan would forever be known as a healing river, where Naaman's leprous skin had become supple and pink once again, and where—by virtue of one man's baptism—the whole world would come to know that Jordan River water can get the nastiest stain out still.

❀ ❀ ❀ ❀ ❀ ❀ ❀

One evening before sunset, I was reading a book ten yards or so away from the River of Mercy, stealing the last few minutes of sunlight. It was one of those evenings when you half-expected to see the mule deer and the silver-gray coyote and the Black bear wrestling playfully in the current and hear the caw of the Steller's jay hushed by the holiness of it all, with the incense of ponderosa pine blessing the dusk in benediction.

"Yeeeeehawwwww." I look up just in time to see a young man in denim cut-offs jackknifing into a deep pool of the river. His scruffy beard and thin white legs and bony frame caked in mud made him appear to be a mountain madman come down for his semi-annual bath. He slapped around for a while, acclimating to the frigid water, yipping and yapping like he had nothing to do with his being there. And then, as quickly as he had jumped in, something jumped out of him, for he began to float, light and feather-like, as if the river had claimed that which he wanted to leave behind.

I left the man to himself, not wanting to intrude on his solitude; and as I made my way back to my campsite and a bowl of hearty stew and a cup of wine, I heard the man humming in the distance. It was a soft hymn of some sort, with the merest hint of an echo, and I knew it was not the hard granite canyon wall that it was bouncing off of but the heart of God, healing and welcoming and whimsical.

This mountain man, whoever he was, was being washed clean in the river named Mercy. So will we all be.

Why Do I Let Myself Worry?

There is a tavern in the small farming town of Tulelake, California, called "The Homestead." It has a long, mahogany bar with ten or twelve swivel stools in front of it and a dusty old pool table in the back. Off in the corner there is an old jukebox filled with dusty Tammy Wynette, Marty Robbins, and Tex Ritter LPs. Friday night is Ladies' Night. They wheel out the karaoke machine, and leather-skinned wives and daughters, bathed in purple light, serenade their tobacco-chewing husbands and boyfriends until three in the morning. It was on a Friday night one summer that my aunts and uncles and brothers and sisters, their wives and husbands, and I assembled at The Homestead. We walked through the door on the night before we were to bury my mother. In true Irish fashion, we had decided to welcome the dawn with a wake not unlike those celebrated on the old sod for hundreds of years.

The old watering hole was crowded that night. It took the train of us five minutes to weave our way to the back, where we put some tables and chairs together and settled in for a night of singing and dancing and stitching stories together that would in the end leave us laughing and crying in equal measure.

It seemed to be the right place to be, in a tavern surrounded by farmers who knew something of the seasons of growing things: of seed and water and sun; of the green of early spring and the ripe of autumn corn and barley; of the harvest; of the pall of white snow over the fields that slows the beat of the heart and adds an extra layer of skin to chilly bones; of the tilling of the wet soil in the new year. They knew something of the rhythms of life that accommodate the inevitability of dying and death.

❖ ❖ ❖ ❖ ❖ ❖ ❖

I went up to the barkeep and ordered the first couple pitchers of beer, and a frazzled woman in a checkered shirt and blue jeans and leather boots leaned over and inspected me, dressed as I was in an unbuttoned roman collar and a Joseph A. Bank charcoal-gray suit. She had watched us as we came in, nary a one of us donning a cowboy hat or sporting cowboy boots.

"What's going on?" she asked lazily, and, God is my witness, she was chewing tobacco. I wondered if this was a typical Tulelake pick-up line, and if I should respond. Do I tell the truth, that we have just left Holy Cross Church having prayed the rosary for my recently departed mother, or do I make something up, lest I be drawn into a long and tedious discussion with this fuddled woman? ("Just travelin' through, ma'am, just travelin' through," I imagined myself saying with the faintest hint of a country drawl, but it didn't seem right, what with Mom's body lying there in the sanctuary of the church and her voice still ringing in my ear: Pat, you *better* tell the truth!)

So I told her the truth, all of it. One word tripped over the other and maternal biography slipped into hagiography. After five minutes or so of sharing with this stranger the joy and the sadness of the last few days and how proud my mom and dad would be of us, that not once in the last three days have we had too much to drink or argued or fought, I realized that she had not moved the entire time. She had been staring at me with rheumy eyes and her chew-stained lips slightly opened, as if she had just witnessed the landing of an alien ship in her potato field. I had said too much. I put a cap on my story with, "and now we are here to have a good ol' fashioned Irish wake!"

She continued to stare and then abruptly turned to her beer and took a long guzzle. Wiping her chin and staring straight ahead, her face turned cold. "What do you think I am?" she said with a tinge of tart on her curled lower lip. "You think I'm ignorant?" And I realized she thought I had been feeding her a line and was none too happy about it. So much for the truth, Mom.

❖ ❖ ❖ ❖ ❖ ❖ ❖

That night at The Homestead was one of those rare nights of peace, when a smile really meant something and the spoken word dripped with earnestness. Death had carried us to a hidden corner of a room cast in deep shadow, daring us to weep all hope away. But all it really succeeded in doing was make us push the darkness away with our soulful singing.

It was rather daring of us, looking back on it, but our choices were limited. It may be one of our species' greatest strengths, this almost natural predilection when faced with darkness to stare it down with defiance until it slinks away, surrendering to the dawn. And that's what my family did that night: We clinked our glasses together in toast to life, even as we tended to our wounded hearts.

Keats, in his great poem *Endymion* wrote, "To Sorrow / I bade good-morrow, / And thought to leave her far away behind; / But cheerly, cheerly, / She loves me dearly. / She is so constant to me, and so kind." It was many years after that evening at The Homestead that I read those words, and it struck me that sorrow and grief betray a kind of joy that blossoms only after it has been watered with tears…lots of them. I sat in the dark corner of the tavern that night sipping on a beer and throwing pretzels at unsuspecting siblings, and all around me there was unfolding what can only be described as a victory celebration.

Wizened old men in loose fitting Levis shot pool and played poker with toothless grins, chuckling at jokes they must have first told each other in high school. Unattached ranchers and farmers in sweaty shirts and slick-backed hair shared drags of cigarettes and talked about irrigation and pesticides while surveying the dance floor with the regularity of a lighthouse. Young lovers held hands as they swayed to the music of Jimmy Buffett; and the barkeep swatted flies and under-aged customers away with deadly accuracy. And my brothers and sisters and aunts and uncles and in-laws laughed and sang, as if Mom were still there, alive and breathing in her menthol cigarette smoke and the musty air.

❀ ❀ ❀ ❀ ❀ ❀ ❀

It was around midnight, and a gentle hum descended upon the tavern as table talk turned more intimate. Lights were dimmed and the jukebox stood silent. A woman in her early seventies with an ill-fitting, tilting wig made her way to the wooden platform. She sat on a stool and wrapped her bony hands around the microphone as the song began on the karaoke. It was Patsy Cline's song "Crazy." I remember thinking that she was the genuine article. Her voice had the rasp of a three-packs-a-day habit, and she couldn't quite hit the high notes, but that really didn't seem to matter. "Worry...why do I let myself worry? Wonderin'...what in the world did I do? Oh, crazy...for thinkin' that my love could hold you. I'm crazy for tryin' and crazy for cryin' and I'm crazy for lovin' you."

She was weathered and wrinkled and worn down by life....

But she was there, and in her own way she gave tribute to all of us who dared to sing long into the night.

I sat there transfixed, struck by her bravery, her audaciousness. This woman, with years of tryin' and cryin' behind her, still spoke from her heart of love in the presence tense. Crazy. In her own small way, she stood with us as my family stared down the darkness together. She was weathered and wrinkled and worn down by life, and yet she held on—maybe from one night to the next—with only a song to keep her going. But she was there, and in her own way she gave tribute to all of us who dared to sing long into the night.

I don't know what it is about us human beings that gives us the power and permission to hang on, but I have seen enough of it in my life to know that it has something to do with the human spirit brushing up against the spirit of God. It is the stuff of faith, a tilting wig, raspy, three-packs-a-day, karaoke kind of faith.

That June evening eighteen years ago, I wanted that night of peace to last forever, like Peter, James, and John wanted the experience to last forever when they climbed the mountain and saw Jesus transfigured in all his glory. Strangely enough, I felt a kind of gratitude as I made my way home that night, for I had found myself in the company of many who had suffered and not been defeated, all of us bathed in the light of mercy that sees us beyond the momentary darknesses of our lives.

Fat Baby

Before she was a teacher, my sister Julie was a lawyer, a public defender in Multnomah County, Oregon. And before she was an attorney, she was Fat Baby, the youngest of our family of nine brothers and sisters. Dad had given her the nickname soon after she was brought home from the hospital. I remember the day in October of 1964 when she was born. Dad drove my sister Margaret and me to the hospital and told us—three and four years old respectively—to wait in the station wagon while he ran in to see how our mother was doing. This was his tenth trip to the Eden Hospital maternity ward in eleven years. He knew the drill.

Dad came out a little while later to announce that we had a new baby sister. Margaret cheered gleefully, knowing even at three years of age that now she was united with a younger sister. The delicate balance of power in the Hannon household would most assuredly tilt in her favor. I was rooting for a younger brother for the same reason and slumped back in my seat disappointed. This was my mother and father's tenth child. Eleven months earlier (on my fourth birthday) they had lost a child, James Joseph, who died at birth. I figured this was my last shot at shedding my lowly status as the youngest son, and now my fate was settled for good.

Julie was one plump butterball of a baby, so unlike the rest of us, who were born scrawny and colicky, grateful to be alive. For the first year, she was the belle of the ball. Jack loved to put lipstick on her when Mom wasn't looking, Margaret played with her toes and got her to squeal, forging a sibling bond that would be unbreakable, and we all fought over who got to take her out in the stroller.

One day Dad came home from work and asked, "Where's the fat baby?" and the name stuck. Sometimes she could be found stuffed in the clothes hamper in the upstairs hallway or perched tenuously on the branch of one of our backyard trees with a couple brothers holding a stretched blanket below telling her it was okay to jump. Sometimes we folded her up with the dog in the hide-a-bed in the rumpus room. We put her through the paces in her early years and found her acceptable.

Julie grew up to be a fighter, and she won most of the battles. She shed her baby fat and turned out to be a rather slender—if not delicate—slight-figured girl. Cursed with tiny fists, she understood her survival rested with her tongue, sharpened and—let's admit it—forked. To this day our two youngest sisters, Margaret and Julie, frighten my brothers and me. Margaret can, if sufficiently provoked, beat any of us into next week. Julie, even when not provoked, can, with the clipping word and cutting phrase, lyrical and almost poetic in its delivery, reduce any of us to quivering Jell-O. "I had to have been adopted," she often says.

❀ ❀ ❀ ❀ ❀ ❀ ❀

I remember sitting in a courtroom one time watching Julie in action. An attorney for the indigent in Portland, Oregon, she was defending a mother of three who had been caught shoplifting at a department store downtown. The woman was in her middle years—maybe forty—but she looked much older. She bore the countenance of a beaten pup; and during the course of the day I understood why. She and her children lived with her boyfriend, who was addicted to drugs and beat her regularly. She shoplifted because her boyfriend told her to, because if she didn't she'd get beaten again. "Get your sorry ass out of bed and do something useful," he'd say, and she knew what he meant. The money she got from selling the clothes she stole fed both his habit and her children. From any angle, this young woman's life appeared insignificant and was seemingly unworthy of anyone's attention. Had my sister not chosen to stand next to her, clearly this woman would have had to face the darkness of her sad life all alone.

Julie was masterful in the courtroom that day. She proffered a creative and daring and honest defense, an argument driven by the facts of the case: This woman's culpability was certainly mitigated by her boyfriend's threats. It was as if he were there next to her in the department store with a bat poised to strike if she didn't do what he told her. She feared for her safety and the safety of her children. She likened her client to a beautiful bird in a cage whose door was wide open but who was so beaten and abused that she was simply too afraid to fly away. The assistant district attorney later complimented Julie (something assistant district attorneys rarely do), because that particular defense had never really been tried before in such a case.

What I remember now is the face of my sister as she spoke to the jury during her closing argument. It was the face of utter confidence and conviction. She believed in her client when no one else would. I remember her voice and her words of fire and ferocity. I remember her fist pounding the podium with calm, persistent pleading, as if her very life depended on her convincing the jurors that her client was really and truly innocent.

She would walk away handcuffed or set free knowing that there was someone on this planet who believed in her.

❀ ❀ ❀ ❀ ❀ ❀ ❀

Frederick Buechner once wrote, "Compassion is sometimes the fatal capacity for feeling what it is like to live inside somebody else's skin. It is the knowledge that there can never really be any peace and joy for me until there is peace and joy finally for you too." Julie, at some point in her life, must have come to a similar insight. It was what drove her that day. Her life was inextricably linked to the life of the young woman sitting next to her at the defense table.

I'd like to think that Julie learned this growing up, that we, her brothers and sisters, taught her something of compassion. Maybe in an indirect way we did. She grew up knowing what it was like to be the underdog. Her first nascent memory might very well have been of me or one of her other brothers reaching into her crib and, with wicked smiles on our faces, putting her in the upstairs linen closet with Tiger the cat and Bambi the dog. Every day for Julie in those early years was an adventure in survival. Would she make it to another day? Well, let's just see! She knew early on that the world could be a harsh and unforgiving place for the weak and vulnerable. Faced with the choice of playing the victim or standing with the victim, she chose the tougher course. She became an advocate.

I will always remember the face of the young woman—my sister's client—sitting in her chair as Julie finished her closing argument. Tears ran down her astonished face as it dawned on her that here was, finally, one other human being willing to fight for her when she was too weak to fight for herself, a voice strong and clear when she could not speak herself.

To say I was proud of Fat Baby that day would be an understatement. Actually, I was in awe. Looking at these two women—one who stood charged with thievery and the other pleading her case—you could not tell where one ended and the other began. Their fates were joined. I remember thinking at the time that the eventual verdict, whatever it was, was secondary, almost incidental. The woman standing accused had won. She would walk away handcuffed or set free knowing that there was someone on this planet who believed in her.

❀ ❀ ❀ ❀ ❀ ❀

Through his entire passion, Jesus clung to the belief that God would never abandon him. God never did. It is this image of God—the advocate, the lawyer who stands by us when no one else will, the One who is our strength when we are weak—that gives us courage to hang on and believe that when our backs are against the wall there will be someone standing with us, someone who by his or her presence tells us—with conviction—we do not have to face the darkness alone.

Untie Her and Let Her Go Free

Letting the pigeon loose in the church was the last straw. The week before, Pam had snuck in a cat wrapped in a blanket and the week before that a scruffy mutt of a dog that hobbled on three legs. But when a rather frightened gray pigeon flapped its wings and ascended to the top of the purple banner hanging in the sanctuary during the opening song at mass, perilously close to the presider's chair I might add, we knew something had to be done. Pam, the Doctor Doolittle of the Downtown Chapel, had to be stopped. Father Berg, the pastor, and I came up with a plan while we guided the panicky pigeon out the chapel door with the help of a ladder and a big broom. While we gathered the feathers the bird had left behind and Pam sat in the front pew quietly talking to herself about how the dove is a sign of the Holy Spirit, the priest and I conversed loud enough for Pam to hear.

"I don't know, I think that bird was pretty frightened," Father Berg began. "I thought it was going to die right there at communion."

"Yeah, I thought the same thing," I returned. "I'm just glad we were able to get the bird out before it had a heart attack. Did you see the terror in that bird's eyes?"

Pam stopped talking about the Holy Spirit and listened intently. Her face grew more worried and alarmed. Second only to Jesus Christ himself, it was the stray cat or the lost dog or, in this case, the pirated pigeon that captured Pam's heart. It began to dawn on her that she might very well have traumatized one of God's little creatures.

"Maybe we should ask Pam not to come back to the chapel for a little while, until she can show us that she can leave the animals outside," I suggested.

"Hmmm. You may be right, Father Pat," the pastor admitted. Both of us were looking over at Pam now, seeing if anything was registering. Something had, for Pam's face was sunken and she was protesting very quietly, like a child being banned from the television set. Keeping Pam away from the chapel, from sitting in the front pew as she always did, interrupting the homily with comments like, "Yes, Jesus!" or "Praise Jesus

Christ!" or "I love you, Jesus!" Well, she would die if she couldn't come to mass every day.

"Pam, are you going to bring animals in the church again?" the pastor asked her.

"Praise Jesus Christ, never again!" Pam reassured us. With that promise tucked neatly away, Pam departed with a smile on her sweet face. Later that afternoon I saw her by the bus stop on the corner, bending the ear of some man in a blue suit holding tightly to his brief case, telling him about how much Jesus loved him and how Jesus freed him from sin and death.

Everyone loved Pam. She heard voices and saw spirits and talked to trees and said things that often made no sense whatsoever. Underneath rags of cotton and polyester and castaway wool, however, was pure and unfiltered generosity. We were all drawn to her charismatic outbursts at mass and her bus stop evangelizing. She had the innocent face and the sweet, soft voice of an angel, albeit one whose wings had become bent and bruised. Not yet able to catch the next breeze to heaven, Pam remained earthbound, tethered to our little corner of the planet.

❀ ❀ ❀ ❀ ❀ ❀ ❀

The details may never be known, but several weeks after the pigeon episode, Pam was brutally beaten up in a small patch of woods a mile or so out of Portland. She returned to us after mending in the hospital, appearing one Sunday morning bound in bandages, her face covered in a shroud of sadness. Something had changed and it was terrible. From then on, Pam sat in the back of the church as quiet as a church mouse. She ran from dogs and hid in abandoned storefront porches, hunched over, her slight frame packed away by sweaters and jackets and scarves and fat gloves. Before the beating, Pam would try to receive communion at all the masses on Sunday, even after we told her once a day was sufficient. After she came back to us, Pam stayed in the back, eyes closed, lips sealed tight, the line of communicants passing by her each time.

Parishioners tried to reach her. One man named Peter used to sit next to her and put his big arms around her and try to nudge her to the altar, but nothing worked. Folks kept quiet vigil with her, telling her every now and then how beautiful she was, telling her how much Jesus loved her. I remember thinking that maybe, just maybe, I might grab myself a pigeon and let it loose in the chapel, thinking that would bring Pam back from the grave. Nothing seemed to reach her.

It was a Wednesday in Lent, several months later, and as was the custom at the Downtown Chapel we celebrated the sacrament of the Anointing of the Sick after mass. Ask anyone in that parish what that faith community's mission is and they will tell you, "To heal the heart of Portland." And so every Wednesday after the 4:30 mass, folks from the neighborhood would emerge from their hovels and gather together to be bathed in healing oil with those who occupied expensive offices in the high-rise buildings downtown. That day, there were sixty-five or seventy people gathered around the altar. Only Pam sat in a pew, back in the corner.

We were gathered in a circle, holding hands, praying for healing, when a spry old man named Charlie stopped everything. A little weed of man, barely five feet tall, he reminded me of Popeye (without the muscles or the spinach). Charlie spent most of his adult life as a hobo, earning his stripes on tracks connecting most of the western states. Charlie started muttering to himself, saying things like, "Lord, you have to do something about this…. What? You really want me to do that? Well, Lord (Charlie was rubbing the stubble on his chin at this point), I don't think I can do that. What if she bites me?" Finally, Charlie looked up at me, shrugged his shoulders, and said, "Father, hold your horses one little second." And with that he made his way back to Pam.

A heated conversation ensued. Pam wasn't budging. Charlie stopped pleading with her and held her, his small arms couldn't even reach all the way around the living, breathing ball of fabric shaking in the shadow of the chapel. He was speaking in her ear, God only knows what. "Whispering sweet nothings" is the only thing Charlie would reveal when asked later what he had said to Pam. Three, four minutes passed; our broken circle waited. Finally, Charlie and Pam made their way up to the altar, one holding the other with such tenderness that it made me pause and enjoy the pure loveliness of human beings.

First Pam took off her gloves, then her sunglasses, and then her knitted cap. After that she removed her yellow parka, then her windbreaker. Then she shed one sweater, then another, then a third. Hands reached over to help her climb out of the clothes she had been buried in. After the sweaters, she peeled off three shirts. And there she stood before us: a startled woman in a very pretty white cotton dress. She came forward and stood in the circle, her hands outstretched as if they had been freed from shackles and chains. Pam stood in the circle of life, bound by tears of sweet victory. There wasn't a dry eye in the place that early evening, when a humbled priest dipped his fingers in sacred oil and bathed a woman's forehead and blessed her delicate hands while she stood weeping in her white cotton dress. The simple folks of the Downtown Chapel touched Pam and caressed her back to life.

In the face of such pain, the best we can do is what Jesus did: We go and face the tomb and weep.

❋ ❋ ❋ ❋ ❋ ❋

People sometimes wonder if Jesus really did raise Lazarus from the dead. I have absolutely no doubt that he did, because he did it again that Wednesday in a small chapel in the heart of a Pacific Northwest town. The speaker in Carl Sandburg's poem "Losers" once confessed that if he ever came upon the tomb of Jonah he would sit and stay there for a while. For, he said, "I was swallowed one time deep in the dark and came out alive after all."

Maybe, in the face of such pain, the best we can do is what Jesus did: We go and face the tomb and weep. In all the gospel accounts, this is the only time we hear of Jesus crying. With eyes filled with tears, he stared down death, and it was death that blinked. Lazarus emerged from the tomb. "Untie him, and let him go free," Jesus said as he wiped the tears from his eyes. For on that day, death would not have the last word. No, the last word that day must have been the word that Charlie heard when we gathered in the circle, except the pronoun was different: "Untie her, and let her go free." And that day, Pam did go free. She was scarred and scatter-brained, clinging lightly to sanity. But she was alive.

One day, a long, long time ago, Jesus raised his good friend Lazarus from the grave. I know. I was there.

SIX

The Wind-Swept Plains
Mercy in Plain View

Jesus came down with them
and stood on a level place,
With a great crowd of his disciples
and a great multitude of people
from all Judea, Jerusalem,
and the coast of Tyre and Sidon….
And all in the crowd were trying to touch him,
for power came out from him
and healed all of them.
Then he looked up at his disciples and said:
"Blessed are you who are poor,
for yours is the kingdom of God.
Blessed are you who are hungry now,
for you will be filled.
Blessed are you who weep now,
for you will laugh.
Blessed are you when people hate you,
and when they exclude you,
revile you,
and defame you
on account of the Son of Man.
Rejoice in that day and leap for joy,
for surely your reward is great in heaven."

Luke 6

Life in the Vast Lane

In his 1885 work, *Ranching in the Bad Lands,* Theodore Roosevelt observed, "The character of this rolling, broken, plains country is everywhere much the same." He continued:

> It is a high, nearly treeless region, of light rainfall, crossed by streams which are sometimes rapid torrents and sometimes merely strings of shallow pools. In places it stretches out into deserts of alkali and sage brush, or into nearly level prairies of short grass, extending for many miles without a break; elsewhere there are rolling hills, sometimes of considerable height; and in other places the ground is rent and broken into the most fantastic shapes, partly by volcanic action and partly by the action of water in a dry climate. These latter portions form the famous Bad Lands. Cotton-wood trees fringe the streams or stand in groves on the alluvial bottoms of the rivers; and some of the steep hills and canyon sides are clad with pines or stunted cedars. In the early spring, when the young blades first sprout, the land looks green and bright; but during the rest of the year there is no such appearance of freshness, for the short bunch grass is almost brown, and the gray-green sage bush, bitter and withered-looking, abounds everywhere, and gives a peculiarly barren aspect to the landscape.

For Roosevelt, the Badlands of North Dakota was his salvation. He had a ranch not too far from the town of Medora and went there every chance he could. Over a period of years, those Badland nights, dry and cool and soothing under a vast eternal sky, acted as a salve to his wounded soul after the death of his first wife Alice. "When my heart's dearest died," he wrote in a memorial soon after her death, "the light went from my life forever." And though the sadness and melancholy never departed the guarded and outwardly cheerful Roosevelt, time spent on the northern plains always refreshed his flagging spirit.

"I grow very fond of this place," he wrote in an unpublished journal, "and it certainly has a desolate, grim beauty of its own, that has a curious fascination for me…. In the evening I love to sit out in front of the hut and see the hard, gray outlines [of the buttes] gradually growing soft and purple as the flaming sunset by degrees softens and dies away."

There is something authentic and true about wide open spaces, what Roosevelt called "the lonely rolling prairie and broken lands." There among the jack rabbit, the prairie dog, the sage hen, and white buck-tail, and with the soft twitter of the cliff swallow to serenade him, Teddy Roosevelt must have made his peace with God. Hemingway would put it this way, "The world breaks everyone and afterward many are strong in the broken places." There in the Badlands, in the "broken lands" as Roosevelt called it then, he became strong in the broken places.

❊ ❊ ❊ ❊ ❊ ❊ ❊

Near old Highway 10 that connects Medora to Beach, North Dakota, my sister Sally pulled her Fleetwood Sports Jamboree recreational vehicle into Red Rock Campground. It was around nine o'clock in the evening. She, my sister Mary, and a bunch of my nieces and nephews had driven out to Chicago one week in late June of 1999 to pick me up for a summer holiday. After the Fourth of July weekend, we pulled out of the Notre Dame High School parking lot and commenced our week-long journey west to Portland along Interstate 94 with a much anticipated scheduled stop in the Badlands.

After a few days on the road we had made it to North Dakota, and it was as Teddy Roosevelt had described it. There was an austere beauty to the rugged and sweeping terrain. I tell you, as I stepped out of the RV and filled my lungs with Badlands air, my first thought was: *I can breathe here.* My sisters and the kids ran off to the Dairy Queen we had passed on the way in, and I went for a walk. For two hours I took long, deep breaths and it melted away: the worry and fatigue and the residue of the past year—my first at Notre Dame High School—that was mostly marked by anxiety and melancholy. *I can breathe here.*

Wide open spaces and a starry night will, if you give them permission, bring you to tears. It had been a long, long time since I had seen the sweep of the Milky Way galaxy from our planetary perch (I being a city boy most of my life). To think that we are on a planet spinning on its axis at the speed of around a thousand miles an hour and hurtling in space around the sun at sixty-seven thousand miles an hour is enough to make you queasy. Seeing the stretch of our own puny galaxy—populated by tens of billions of stars—and realizing that we are all, planets and stars, moving in unison like dancers twirling to a waltz on some orbit in our little corner of the universe at over a million miles an hour, I tell you it was a humbling and exhilarating experience. There I was, in the Badlands of North Dakota, in the middle of nowhere—and everywhere—a witness to the grandeur and grace of it all.

✦ ✦ ✦ ✦ ✦ ✦ ✦

Later that evening, with the younger kids fast asleep and under the watchful eye of their elder cousins, my sisters and I went to town and found ourselves at The Backyard Bar having a late-night snack of cheese-fries and Cokes. I noticed two swinging doors off to the right, the kind that used to grace the entrance to the saloons of the Old West. They opened to a small card-playing room. I peeked through and saw an older woman sitting by herself behind a blackjack table. She could have been the lost twin of my Grandma Lighthouse. She had the same soft white curly hair, the same vintage light-blue Cat Eye glasses, the same loose skin on the neck, and the same healthy girth squeezed into a print dress like the one my grandma often wore.

The woman shuffled and dealt cards with the dexterity of a Vegas dealer, which convinced me that she must be the great-aunt on my mom's side that no one talked about. We played blackjack, this woman and I, until two in the morning. Blackjack dealers, I discovered, are not unlike barbers and bartenders and priest-confessors: In their presence—even as they are busy plying their respective trades of trimming, pouring, absolving, and card dealing—you feel free to unpeel the layers of your life, confident that what you say to them remains with them. We had a great conversation, this woman and I, every word of which escapes my

We are like the stars

of the Milky Way,

twirling in time,

moving gracefully together

across the dance floor

we call the universe,

pulled and driven

by a mysterious force

that links us to the same

amazing journey.

memory. What remained was the intersection of my story with hers. It left me with the profound sense that none of us is ever really alone in this world.

Our paths had crossed only briefly. Though I can't speak for her, by the time I left I was not only thirty bucks richer (so maybe she wasn't my long lost aunt after all). But I was fortified by the truth that if you are fortunate to find a place that affords you the view you can see clearly enough that we're all connected. All of our stories are like single notes in one never-ending song. We are like the stars of the Milky Way, twirling in time, moving gracefully together across the dance floor we call the universe, pulled and driven by a mysterious force that links us to the same amazing journey.

All this I saw in plain view in the Badlands of North Dakota, a place that at first blush seems severe and unaccommodating but with a little patience helps you see what is too often hidden. "The broken lands," Teddy Roosevelt called it, a wide open space of intersection and connection, a work of God's mercy carved into the northern plains that makes us all strong in our broken places.

Candles in Dark Places

We had come from Amsterdam, my sisters and I, and were now making our way up the Avenue des Champs Elysees in Paris. It was early August, and those Parisians who could afford it had already fled the city and the humidity for the more pleasant summer breezes of the south of France, so the boulevard that led majestically to the Arc de Triumphe that morning was, for the most part, deserted. Two days later, while praying in the Cathedral of Notre Dame, I had an encounter with a father and his little boy that I have never forgotten. But to understand the significance of that day in the cathedral, I need you to step back a little and see the bigger picture.

It was the summer of 1989, and my sisters Mary, Margaret, Julie, and I had taken a ten-day trip to Europe. The Monica Hannon Victory Tour, we called it. I don't know whose idea it was, but at the time it seemed like the right thing to do. Let's go to Europe, one of us said; in memory of Mom, another one piped. And so we went. It was early August before we were all able to secure passports and plane tickets and permission from our spouses or religious superior. Julie, the youngest and as yet unattached, was the one who had been to Europe already, having spent a year abroad studying in Salzburg, Austria. She was to be our guide.

Our pre-trip planning was anything but painstaking and arduous. We would fly into Frankfurt, Germany, on July 30 and fly out of Paris on August 10. Oh, yes, we would have a rental car, a spry 1986 Renault. That was it. We knew we would start by seeing a cousin who lived with her Bavarian husband and child in the town of Holzkirchen, located between Munich to the north and the Bavarian Alps to the south. We knew we would visit Salzburg and help Julie relive the days when she had survived weekends on sauerkraut and raw onions. The rest of the trip would be an unscheduled day-to-day adventure until we reached Paris.

The last night before departing Holzkirchen, while enjoying a few pints of the town's finest Pilsner, we decided, definitively, that we would head north to Amsterdam. It had canals and coffee shops and museums and churches and parks, something for everyone! But I wanted to go because Anne Frank once lived there and because Van Gogh and Rembrandt painted there and because Spinoza philosophized there. Yes, Amsterdam beckoned.

Amsterdam almost didn't happen. We were sitting in a McDonald's in Luxemburg City. In the adjacent booth, a family of gypsies was scarfing down burgers and fries; the youngest, an infant, fed from her mother's exposed breast. Margaret had gone to the restroom, which gave Julie and me the chance to convince Mary that northern Italy would be a much more enjoyable destination. We kept on repeating the city names of Milan, Florence, Venice, assured that the sound of their names alone would paint for her an irresistible picture of gondola rides at sunset and dinners along the Elsa River and wines from the vineyards of Lombardy and Veneto. Instead of heading north, we would simply head south. It'll be a beautiful drive, we tell her.

Mary, you understand, is about as accommodating a person you will ever find on the planet. I think we had her at, "Mary, we're thinking of maybe…." But Margaret, on the other hand, is rather strong-willed. She's generous to a fault, open-minded, compassionate, a sucker for the stray and the straggler; but once she gets something into her head, she's going to do it, come hell or high water, so to speak.

"The hell we are," she said when we informed her of our unanimous decision. It didn't matter if it was three to one. Apparently this was not a democracy. She was heading north and that was that. If we wanted to come along, that would be fine. We went to Amsterdam.

❀ ❀ ❀ ❀ ❀ ❀

I'm glad we did. There we met Ursulla, whom we nicknamed "The Mad Dutchwoman" because she was certifiably crazy. I'm not kidding. We found her name in the *International Herald Tribune*'s section advertising cheap lodging. She gave us directions from the central train station to her place, and when she saw us in our rickety Renault at maybe forty yards, she ran up to us, *while we were still moving*, pounded on the hood of our car, and yelled to us really loud, "You stop NOW!"

We stayed out later than we wanted those nights in Amsterdam because we didn't want to be cornered by Ursulla and have her tell us yet again why she hated Americans and why her life was mired in misery and why she never should have married her husband of forty years whom she never really loved (and who, by the way, never spoke a word to us during our entire stay). She smoked unfiltered cigarettes (rolled them herself) and sang one song of lamentation after another, peppered with profanity.

One of our Amsterdam nights, however, I stayed in because I had a headache. Ursulla sat at the edge of my bed in the attic room where we were staying and cried, actually cried, for an hour. I think she had recently been arrested and sentenced to a year of community service because some recent guests (American) had been caught doing lascivious things on her balcony.

We paid up the night before we left, and early that next morning we snuck down the steep Dutch staircase of the house (waving goodbye to the husband on the second landing, who was sitting at the kitchen table having a peaceful pre-dawn cup of coffee); it was something right out of the movie *The Great Escape*. We hugged each other as each of us made it to the car and freedom. Then it was on to Paris and a cathedral and a candle in a corner.

❖ ❖ ❖ ❖ ❖ ❖ ❖

Up until my twenty-ninth year, I never once lit a candle in a church. As a kid I used to think that you had to be at least seventy or seventy-five to enjoy the privilege, judging from the steady stream of whiskered old men and pious old ladies that wove its way to the candle stands under the statues of Mary and Jesus at Our Lady of Grace Church in my hometown. By the time I was a teenager and dispensed with that myth—having realized that as a child anyone over the age of thirty looked to be seventy or seventy-five—I didn't stick around after mass long enough to entertain the notion. Besides, the idea of paying my hard-earned newspaper-delivery profits to light a candle made no sense at all to my young brain.

No, I left the candle lighting to others, impressed by the way they took a taper and borrowed the flame from another candle to ignite their own and so extend by an inch the territory of light that graced the corners of the church.

It was as if whatever they were praying for, or whomever they were praying for, required more than whispered words; it was prayer begging for something tangible and real, something they could see and touch and feel, so that when they went to mass again they could glance over and see evidence of their faith, flickering in the corner, in the territory of light.

So there I was, in the Cathedral of Notre Dame in Paris, having carried with me across the ocean the heavy and deep sorrow of my mother's recent death in my heart. I did what the faithful and the fickle have done in that cathedral for seven hundred years: I lit a candle. I don't know exactly why I did it, except that maybe—because I was so shaken and lost at the time—I needed evidence of my faith, something that told me that I still believed in God, that my mother, though dead, was not defeated by death. I lit the candle the way I had seen it done a thousand times before, and then I made my way to a pew in the middle of the cathedral, knelt there for a while, and prayed.

I needed evidence of my faith, something that told me that I still believed in God, that my mother, though dead, was not defeated by death.

❋ ❋ ❋ ❋ ❋ ❋

Soon there came a young man dressed in a black suit, with a little boy at his side also dressed in a black suit. They made their way to one of the statues in the corner under which a rack of candles stood. Lit candles poured light into all the dark places of the alcove and seemed to breathe life into the stone and the marble and the plaster statue. The father raised the son and placed a lit taper into his hand and guided the boy to one of the unlit candles. The child lit the candle and the father and son knelt for a short while. The father crossed himself and the son, observing this, crossed himself. Finally they got up to leave, but before they did the father reached into his coat pocket and retrieved a photograph. He gave it to his son, who placed it in the outstretched hand of the statue. Later

I went up to the statue and discovered that it was a picture of the father and son and the boy's mother in a boat on a lake somewhere, all of them smiling at the camera. The picture could have been taken a week before.

In a cathedral of saints carved from stone and marble and etched into stained glass of purple and blue and red; in a cathedral dedicated to the mother of Jesus, the lady of so many sorrows; in a cathedral protected on the outside by five thousand gargoyles, gothic chimera poised on the edges of the high towers and along the outside wall to pounce on anything evil; the young man took his child into his arms and walked away. They walked past me. The young boy's head was buried in his father's neck as he clung to his father's shoulders. I could see clearly that the boy of three, maybe four, was crying. His father, you could tell, was doing all he could to comfort his son.

I suspected there were at least two boys in the cathedral that day whose hearts had been broken by the deaths of their mothers.

❖ ❖ ❖ ❖ ❖ ❖ ❖

I turned around to see if my sisters were around and finally noticed that scores of people surrounded me, kneeling and sitting and praying. Faces like mine, focused on some distant point far ahead, waiting for the bridegroom to come over the horizon. Eyes like mine, focused on the One who promised to bring glad tidings to those who were carrying heavy burdens. Lips like mine, moving, mumbling, and offering prayers that rose like incense, dismissive of the gravity of grief that pressed down upon their saddened souls.

We were all in it together: The hundred people surrounding me, the father and son who left behind a token of love, Ursulla the Mad Dutchwoman and her hapless husband, the gypsy family from a Luxemburg McDonald's, and my own family were all in this together. I knew then what Holy Communion really signifies and how it has this miraculous ability to bring us all together in mercy—the poor, the hungry, the sorrowful. It reminds us that when we light one candle for one person, we're lighting it for everyone.

One Hundred and Three Steps

If you were to ask any of my brothers and sisters what they liked most about staying over at Grandma's house on Trestle Glen in Oakland as kids, they would give you the same answer that I would: sleeping in her bed. Second maybe only to the womb, it was—at least on this side of Paradise—a place of great peace and happiness. Sleeping with Mom and Dad as a child rarely offered such lasting comfort. Dad's feet were too cold, and he snored with such force that family legend has it that as a boy his own brothers made him sleep out in the barn on warm nights, much to the dismay of the cows and the chickens.

Like heaven, Grandma's bed was not so much a place as it was a state of being. On those rare days—usually in the summer—when I got to spend time alone with her at her house, I couldn't wait for nighttime, when she would lay out the last hand of gin rummy, yawn widely, and tell me to brush my teeth. Climbing into her bed and diving under the warm down comforter, I would smile broadly as I buried my face in the feather pillow and took in the sweet smell of talcum. I would fall asleep to the sounds of the ticking of the bedside clock, the barking of the neighbor's dog, and the steady, deep breathing of a wise, old woman. I would wake up the next morning to the sound and smell of frying eggs and bacon. If there were a luckier boy on the planet, I would like to have met him.

Everything else on those summer weekends was prelude to this peace. Hours of hide 'n seek with the kids in the neighborhood, trips to the Dairy Queen for ice cream, expeditions into the back yards of unsuspecting homeowners. For me, it all paled next to the peace in the fledgling soul of a kindergartner as he drifted off to sleep. At the end of my day, adventure always surrendered to the grandmotherly goodnight kiss, the smell of her talcum powder, and the cadence of her ancient breathing. And to think that one summer day I thought I had lost it all.

I was five years old with a five-year-old's appreciation for consequences. I don't remember why I had my grandmother's house keys, but I did. They were a collection of shiny keys on a wide ring that she kept hung on a hook in the kitchen. My summer friends and I probably were using them as a prop for one of our games. Somehow this ring of keys found their way to the bottom of a storm drain, a good four feet or so below the heavy grate at the end of the curb near my grandma's house. My playmates and I put our heads together and decided we needed some kind of long stick to retrieve the ring. I had just the stick. By the front door of my grandma's house, lost among several umbrellas, was an old walking stick that once belonged to my grandpa. I quickly retrieved the old weathered piece of walnut, and we went to work.

Imagine my horror when the stick snapped on the third or fourth try at digging out the keys. The bottom third dangled there like the loose end of a broken arm. My summer friends scurried away like rats off of a sinking ship as I sat there on the curb weighing my options for repair that would be both effective and, more importantly, invisible. I tried glue, scotch tape, and thumb tacks, but nothing worked. By dusk I was dizzy with panic. I can tell you now that what scared me the most was not the licking I fully expected or the look of disappointment I anticipated on my grandma's face when she saw the fractured walking stick. No, it was realizing that I might never get to sleep in her bed again. I simply could not face such an exile.

My heart raced with fury that night, even as its wound was being mended... racing to keep up with the steady beat of God's own heart.

❖ ❖ ❖ ❖ ❖ ❖ ❖

My grandmother lived on a cul-de-sac. Between two neighboring houses was a stone staircase that seemed to climb to heaven itself. It was there that I retreated, choosing to wait at the top of the staircase for divine intervention rather than go inside for dinner. It was the longest journey of my short life. One hundred and three steps to be exact. With each step I felt the weight of my sin grow heavier in my heart. The higher

I climbed, the deeper I sunk. I don't remember how long I sat there, but I remember it got pretty dark. I don't even remember Grandma calling for me. One second I was alone, and the next second she was standing at the foot of the steps below looking up. I didn't even have time to hide the broken walking stick. Her hands were pasted to her hips. She called for me to come down.

"I'M SORRY!" I yelled.

Come down, she repeated.

"I'M SORRY. I'M SORRY!" I repeated.

She began to climb the stairs. A third of the way up, she stopped.

"I'M SORRY," I said.

She recommenced her climb. The closer she got to me, the louder I yelled.

"I'M SORRY!"

Now she stood directly in front of me. I stood up. She took my hand and together we began our descent.

"I'm sorry," I whispered over and over again, holding the broken walking stick in my free hand.

We walked into the house and made our way to the kitchen, where I knew she kept the long leather switch with which I would be disciplined.

"I'm sorry," I said one last time, and tears begin to well up in my eyes.

She sat me down at the kitchen table and served me a big piece of pie.

❀ ❀ ❀ ❀ ❀ ❀

I had fully expected to be sent to bed in the garage that night, to a cot tucked into the corner next to the water heater. Instead she fed me pie and later played gin rummy with me—she even let me win a game—and let me watch TV past my normal bedtime.

Could it be true, I thought. Could she have completely forgotten my transgression? I had been told that sometimes old people forget things, but this seemed too good to be true. When I climbed into her bed that night and listened to the steady, peaceful rhythm of her breathing, it dawned on me that something strange and mysterious was at work, something that a five-year-old's mind simply could not comprehend. My heart raced with fury that night, even as its wound was being mended. It was only until much later in my life that I understood it was racing to keep up with the steady beat of God's own heart. Two hearts beating as one: It was the only thing I remember hearing that night as I drifted off to sleep.

SEVEN

The Long and Lonesome Valley
Alone No More

The LORD is my shepherd,
I shall not want.
He makes me lie down in green pastures;
he leads me beside still waters;
he restores my soul.
He leads me in right paths
for his name's sake.
Even though I walk through the darkest valley,
I fear no evil;
for you are with me;
your rod and your staff—they comfort me.

You prepare a table for me
in the presence of my enemies;
you anoint my head with oil;
my cup overflows.
Surely goodness and mercy shall follow me
all the days of my life,
and I shall dwell in the house of the LORD
my whole life long.

Psalm 23

Rubicon

The wine they drink in Paradise
They make in Haute Lorraine;
God brought it burning from the sod
To be a sign and signal rod
That they that drink the blood of God
Shall never thirst again.

G. K. Chesterton
from *A Cider Song*

February of 1989. The bishop lays hands on me in the sanctuary of St. Clement Church in Hayward, California, and anoints my hands with holy oil. A Holy Cross priest vests me with the white stole and chasuble, signs of the priestly office, and I join the bishop and my brother priests at the altar to make holy the bread and the wine for Eucharist. With my mother in the first pew surrounded by my brothers and sisters and aunts and uncles and cousins and nieces and nephews and parishioners and friends, I celebrate my first mass as a Holy Cross priest. Before the final blessing at the end of mass, I kneel once more before the assembly. My mother comes forward and lays her hands on my head and blesses me. She presses her lips against my ear and tells me she loves me. It is the most important moment in my life. In June—four short months later—she dies of cancer.

❖ ❖ ❖ ❖ ❖ ❖ ❖

July of 1989. I am with my friend and seminary classmate Bob Loughery, and we are riding our bikes through the Napa Valley on a warm summer day along the old Silverado Trail, a thirty-mile road that weaves its way through eucalyptus and oak and California sycamore and coyote brush. Rows and rows of grape vines, meticulously pruned, flank the hillsides, protected by the Mayacamas mountain range that wraps around us. Two of the range's peaks, Mt. St. Helena to the north and Hood Mountain to the west, are compasses for our journey.

Casa Nuestra. Clos du Val. Regusci. Signorelli. We pass one winery after another under the midday sun; it is as if we are biking through Italian Tuscany or French Bordeaux or Spanish Catalonia. Some day soon the grapes will be harvested and then crushed, pressed, fermented, and clarified. Then shall it slumber in barrels or bottles in cool, dry places until in a few years time, having come of age, it will be uncorked and poured and savored. Cabernet Sauvignon, Merlot, Syrah, Gamay Beaujolais, Petit Verdot, Pinot Noir: It answers to many names with a poetic lilt, but it will—if you let it—tell a grand story.

❈ ❈ ❈ ❈ ❈ ❈

June of 2004. I am with my brothers Mike and Jack and their sons. We are at a Cineplex somewhere in the south bay. We have come to see Alexander Payne's film *Sideways*, a comical reflection on the vicissitudes of love and friendship. It is also a touching love letter to the grace and beauty of wine. While on a date, Miles, the protagonist of the story, is talking with Maya, a woman whom he has admired from afar, who pours wine at a restaurant in town. Miles asks her why she is "so into wine."

"I, I like to think about the life of wine…how it's a living thing," she says. "I like to think about what was going on the year the grapes were growing; how the sun was shining; if it rained. I like to think about all the people who tended and picked the grapes. And if it's an old wine, how many of them must be dead by now. I like how wine continues to evolve, like if I opened a bottle of wine today it would taste different than if I'd opened it on any other day, because a bottle of wine is actually alive. And it's constantly evolving and gaining complexity. That is, until it peaks, like your '61. And then it begins its steady, inevitable decline."

After the movie, we go out to dinner, and Jack chooses a very pricy chardonnay from Cakebread Cellars for our meal. We toast Mom and Dad and the family. The wine has a rich, buttery and toasty oak taste to it, and like the sacramental wine that becomes "the blood of God" as

Chesterton put it, the first sip of that chardonnay makes me very, very thankful: thankful for my life, for my family, for just about everything.

❈ ❈ ❈ ❈ ❈ ❈ ❈

March of 2005. To celebrate his fiftieth birthday, Jack rents a limousine for the night that will take him, a couple of his friends, and two of our brothers, Brian and Mike, from his home in the Hayward hills to the Niebaum-Coppola Winery in the Napa Valley fifty miles away. For Jack, the Niebaum-Coppola Winery (re-christened later as Rubicon Estates) is a hint of heaven, a piece of paradise, a place of bliss and grace where God has truly made a home. Not a regular churchgoer, Jack is content to find holiness among those rows of grapevines that drape the Napa Valley and her sister valley across the way, Sonoma. Among the Napa Valley wineries, Niebaum-Coppola is his cathedral.

There is a divine conspiracy that pushes us together. It is a conspiracy so hidden and so subtle that we sometimes don't even know it is happening... until it has.

I fly in from Chicago to surprise Jack, and after an elaborate ruse constructed by my brother Brian that has me hiding behind an SUV three houses away for ten minutes, I jump into the limousine as it begins to pull out. Jack is delighted to see me. We uncork a bottle of champagne and raise a toast in honor of yet another sibling who has bitten the dust of a half-century of life.

We arrive at the winery, and the sun has already begun to set over Mt. St. John, against which the vineyard rests. The early evening is short-sleeved cool and pleasant. Two hundred guests of the winery have arrived already, and there is a palpable feeling of anticipation in the air, for this is the night that they uncork for that year their flagship wine, a 2001 Cabernet Sauvignon aptly named "Rubicon." They took the name from

Roman history, the Rubicon being the ancient river that separated Gaul from Italy; apparently, once you crossed it, you could never go back.

❖ ❖ ❖ ❖ ❖ ❖

It is later in the evening. Many of the guests that night have departed. The hors d'oeuvres have all been eaten and the last of the wine has been poured. My brothers and I are sitting at the water fountain that graces the Italian-style palazzo in front of the winery's main building. We each savor a last glass of Rubicon and fifteen dollar cigars. Few, if any, words are shared; but we are all witnesses to an epiphany that night borne on the wings of a cool Napa valley breeze that carries with it the aroma of rich fertile soil, wisteria, and ripe grape.

Here was what the Hannon boys realized that night: We human beings are never alone. There is a divine conspiracy that pushes us together. It is a conspiracy so hidden and so subtle that we sometimes don't even know it is happening…until it has. Then we discover that we have crossed a line, our Rubicon, and can never go back. Nor would we want to.

Wherever that moment of grace might occur—like that night my brothers and I shared a bottle of Rubicon and reclined under a blanket of stars that lit up the valley and smoked cigars and barely said anything— that is where we want to be. It is rather sneaky of God. We call it God's mercy. It is fine wine indeed.

The Tenderloin

San Francisco itself is art, above all literary art.
Every block is a short story, every hill a novel.
Every home a poem, every dweller within immortal.
That is the whole truth.

William Saroyan

It was the most painful day of my short life to that point. I was thirteen years old. Candy Cunha, the twelve-year-old granddaughter of my neighbor from across the street—and my summer sweetheart—told me she liked Brian Campbell now and wanted to break up with me. She hoped we could still be friends, though. Thanks. Take that knife, *friend*, you know, the one that you inserted into my back, and twist it a little more. My brother Mike always told me you should never date younger women, and, boy, was he right. I sat in my basement bedroom for three days with the curtains drawn, the lights out, one lone candle burning, and a John Denver album playing on the turntable.

One of the fortunate things about growing up in a large family like mine is that you can do something like this without so much as raising an eyebrow. As far as my brothers and sisters were concerned, it meant more food for them at dinnertime. Two days passed before anyone even really noticed I was in lovesick seclusion.

Eventually, of course, I had to reemerge, but it was not without some fanfare. I hit my sisters more, I drew my brothers into stupid arguments, and I dragged out that look of complete and total contempt and disgust that children have perfected over the centuries so they can drive their parents completely mad. *I hope we can still be friends.* It made me want to kick the dog, which I could not really do because our dog was a Chihuahua and it would have caused serious internal injuries, something even I—with all my pain—could not bring myself to do.

I began taking long solitary walks in far off neighborhoods so I wouldn't run into anybody I knew. I walked in the hills that draped our neighborhood till dusk. I walked downtown Castro Valley. I walked in the park. I was thirteen, and already I was developing a poet's appreciation for irony. How could there be so much life out there, brimming over and busting out and breaking through, while I felt so completely empty in here—in my own broken heart, lost as I was in a deep valley of pain? I took it all in, like snapshots from a rusty camera: an ancient couple holding hands on a wooden park bench wrapped in a blanket of sacred silence; a group of boys playing a pickup game of basketball; fathers with their sons in tow heading into Pete's Hardware Store; middle-aged women with floppy summer hats pulling weeds in their gardens and sipping iced tea; twelve-year-old girls at the bowling alley—all of whom looked like Candy Cunha—moving in menacing herds, whispering and pointing and giggling and making me feel miserable.

❖ ❖ ❖ ❖ ❖ ❖ ❖

Late one afternoon, trying to shake off the darkness that covered me like a pall, I carried my tattered and shadowed soul into San Francisco. I had been to San Francisco before, but this marked the first time I had ventured into "The City" by myself. Dad had driven all of us kids in the station wagon once to Haight-Ashbury, the hippie neighborhood of San Francisco, so we would see what drugs and rock and roll could do to our souls. It was 1968, and he was determined to scare us straight. I remember being endlessly fascinated by everything I saw and heard and smelled. To this day, I cannot take in the whiff of incense without thinking of Haight-Ashbury.

Alone in The City, I got lost, of course. It made perfect sense. My innate Irish fatalism set in. I would die there, in the alley next to the liquor store with the iron bars latched to the windows. At my funeral, Candy Cunha would be sitting in the front pew dressed in black, weeping into the lace handkerchief I had pilfered from my mother's dresser and given to her on Valentine's Day. She would be telling everyone gathered there that I was the true love of her life.

To be honest, I was pretty terrified. I was wandering around in the seedy part of town fittingly nicknamed "The Tenderloin." It had all the grace and dignity and beauty of a slice of dead cow. Flop houses and taverns and pawnshops littered the neighborhood, stone and brick monuments to human failure hiding behind neon lights and whitewash paint. It was around five o'clock in the evening, and the blanket of San Francisco fog pushed in from the ocean as the sun made a quick descent behind the Marin Headlands. A cold spirit fell upon The Tenderloin. Arguments drifted out of open windows; impatient motorists honked their horns; doors were slammed; an old stubble-chinned man stumbled out of a saloon, inebriated and dissatisfied and itching for a fight. It's the closest I came to actually wetting my pants, I was so petrified.

In a flash of unexpected and unasked for blessing, dusk turned into dawn and fear surrendered to faith.

Then I heard a howl. It came from an alley as I was passing it, and it made me freeze in my tracks. I stood there as a wino with long white hair emerged, pushing a shopping cart filled with empty cans and bottles. He had piercing blue eyes, the kind that you would swear were looking directly into your soul. The old man was moving at a pretty fast clip, so when he finally saw me he had to put the skids on the shopping cart; otherwise, he would have run right over me. A few loose cans landed at my feet. There we stood, facing each other on the opposite ends of a shopping cart. He must have known by looking at me that at any moment I was going to burst into tears.

The man took his right hand and raised it; and then, with the dignity of a holy saint, he made the sign of the cross over me and blessed me. It was as if God had come down from heaven that very moment and took a street teeming with despair and darkness and transformed it into a cathedral of light. In a flash of unexpected and unasked for blessing, dusk turned into dawn and fear surrendered to faith.

"You're blocking my way, sonny," he said. So I stepped to the side, and he continued on his way.

❖ ❖ ❖ ❖ ❖ ❖ ❖

Making the sign of the cross has never been the same for me after that encounter with the man with the shopping cart. On a lonely hill one dark Friday, Jesus freely handed his life over to the executioner, who dutifully nailed him to a cross. Somehow Jesus understood that the path to true peace, the kind of peace that shatters the deepest darkness, had to go through the cross of sacrifice, which for the whole world has become the greatest sign of God's mercy. If you live long enough, if you dare to love enough, you see the truth in that pretty clearly: The greatest expression of love is born of mercy. This, an alley cat of a man taught me. He carved a cross into the foggy night air, and from his poverty blessed me with the only thing of value he had. Leave it to God to come in such a disguise, delighted that yet another of his beloved children found his way back home. There is no place God will not go to find us, nothing God will not do to bring us back. It is a promise carved on a cross of mercy, on a cross of hope. It is gift and grace, unexpected and often unasked for. In the end, it will be what saves us.

The Territory of Mercy

Every three or four months I accompany Steve, one of the parishioners from the parish here in Colorado Springs, to Cañon City, fifty miles to the south. He is a regular volunteer at the Colorado State Penitentiary located there, a medium-security prison that began first as the Territorial Prison for Colorado. It is the oldest prison in the state.

I go there to hear confessions and celebrate mass with the Catholic inmates. I have to admit that after going through the all-day orientation program before becoming a volunteer prison chaplain, I was more than a little nervous the first time I stepped through the barbed-wire gates of the big house. Paula, the correctional officer who put me through the paces said at the very end of the training day that the chance of my being taken as a hostage is remote. I made a mental note: She failed to say *very* remote.

Prison is the territory of felons. There are murderers and rapists and child molesters there. There are arsonists and kidnappers and drug addicts. *They will try to get you to like them,* Paula told me. *You never want to tell them where you live,* she said. *These are not upstanding citizens; they are in prison because they did bad things.* Paula showed me pictures of shanks—homemade knives—that were originally plastic spoons or pieces of Plexiglas from a prison lunch tray or the metal coil from inside a prison mattress. *They have twenty-four hours a day to think about nothing but how they can get out,* Paula said. *Do you know why they don't let priests and ministers distribute small, pocket-size bibles in the Territorial Prison?* Paula asked. *They'll use the pages from the bible to roll joints. They're the perfect size.*

I go to the Territorial Prison because Steve asked me to many times before I finally said yes. Steve goes down there several times a month to spend time with the Catholic inmates and pray with them. I go because Steve hasn't been knifed or taken hostage. Yet.

❈ ❈ ❈ ❈ ❈ ❈ ❈

We arrive at the front gate to the prison about 6:30 p.m. One of the guards from the front tower leans out the window, checks his clipboard, and buzzes us in. We go through the front door of the prison, where we empty all the contents of our pockets before walking through the metal detector. We get buzzed through another set of locked doors.

We reach the final checkpoint where we sign in and get our temporary badges. It's business as usual for the guard sitting behind the thick bulletproof window in front of us. While he and Steve carry on a conversation, I look out the window and see inmates going from point A to point B. Some are playing basketball on the outdoor court. Others are making their way back to their cellblock. Still others are gathering at the window at the prison infirmary to pick up their medication.

We get buzzed through once more and I am officially, for the first time, walking on prison ground. "Evenin', Pastor," one inmate says to me as we pass by. *They will try to get you to like them,* Paula said. "Good evening," I say, trying to be respectful but not too friendly.

Steve says hello to a number of inmates he obviously knows, and they call him by his first name. This calms my nerves a little. We are now in at the small prison chapel, a plain white-washed cinderblock square building with a cross above the door. We have arrived a little early so I can set up for mass before hearing confessions. "Everything in prison-runs on the hour," Steve tells me. We have fifteen minutes to kill, so I look around the multi-purpose room. I see notices for Catholic mass and for Protestant services, as well as prayer times for Jewish and Muslim inmates. Once a month they even have a service for those who practice Wicca.

The bell rings at the top of the hour, and in a few minutes Catholic inmates begin arriving. Before they can leave their cells, they have to put on a green-colored slip-over shirt indicating that they are going to chapel. I put on my alb and stole and take a seat in the chaplain's office, where I will hear confessions. The door has a big window. *The chance of your being taken as a hostage is remote,* I remember. But not *very* remote.

One inmate after another comes and confesses his sins to me. Almost all of them come in and kneel right in front of me. Some have bibles with them, which are worn and rabbit-eared and underlined. *They have twenty-four hours a day to think about nothing but how they can get out.*

All of them are trying to make sense of their lives. Like recovering addicts (many of them in fact are), they try to own up to their sins without wallowing and drowning in them. It isn't easy.

I listen, intently and intensely. They open up their hearts to me because I wear a purple stole. They open up to me in a way they dare not on the cellblock. One man is blind. Another is a mute. He communicates carefully with a pencil and paper. He is around forty years old but seems to have the spirit of a child. He can't stop smiling. I am no longer thinking about shanks and hostage-taking.

A young man comes in and shows me a picture of his wife and daughter. He gets out in three months. The final inmate comes in. He is huge. Both arms are covered with tattoos. I try to maintain eye contact, but there's one tattoo of the Virgin Mary on his right forearm that I can't seem to stop looking at. She's riding a Harley.

In the large room outside, twenty-five or so inmates are singing up a storm. Steve and another volunteer from the local parish are leading. None of them can sing to save their lives. They are singing on at least three different keys. I'll tell you this, though. You haven't heard "Amazing Grace" until you've heard it sung by a choir of Catholic criminals.

I have spent an hour and a half hearing confessions, so Steve tells me we only have a half hour for mass. Everything runs on the hour. I don't remember, looking back, what the gospel of the day was, but I'm sure I preached about hope, about hanging on, about not giving up. Some of these guys will never get out. Some who are in their twenties will not breathe free air until they're in their sixties. A number of lucky ones will leave soon or be transferred to a lower-security lock-up.

When they come up for Holy Communion, each and every one of them kneels before me, tilts his head, and opens his mouth for the bread they believe will nourish their souls. I want to lift them up and tell them they don't have to grovel before the Lord of Life, that this is a feast of victory; but I'm convinced if I had tried to do this they would have looked at me like I was crazy. They are the worst kind of sinner, and they know it.

❋ ❋ ❋ ❋ ❋ ❋ ❋

I have a new feeling as Steve and I leave the prison that night. I've never had this feeling before. As we get buzzed through the last gate, it dawns on me that I get to leave. I get to climb into a car and drive fifty miles north and pull up to a house and put a key in a lock and open a back door. I get to open a refrigerator and a have a snack of my choosing. I get to watch television and go to bed when I want to. I get to sleep in my own bed and get up in the morning and go to work. The men with whom I had just broken bread, these felons whom God had forgiven and I had absolved, were going back to their cells. They had only five minutes to get there, because everything runs on the hour. I'm not sure what you call the feeling that is a mixture of sadness and relief, but that's the feeling I had.

They forfeited their freedom for a time commensurate to their crime. But when we gathered for Eucharist, they were my brothers.

Prisons are inhumane places. They are built and designed and run so that human persons no longer think of themselves as human persons. Inmates are given a number; their lives are as regimented as caged animals. The one thing that makes us different from all God's creatures—our freedom—is taken away. And maybe that is how it should be. Those men at the Territorial Prison weren't there because they had been caught jaywalking. They forfeited their freedom for a time commensurate to their crime. But when we gathered for Eucharist, they were my brothers.

So I felt a deep sadness for them. I also felt relief, because I was leaving that God-forsaken place. Despair hunkers down in such places. Demons roam freely in such places. I was glad to leave.

Driving back I thought of the people I hadn't met that night: their victims. I thought of those whose lives were irreparably damaged, maybe destroyed, by these men's crimes. I asked myself, *How would you feel if one of them had killed your brother or raped your sister or molested one of your nieces or nephews? How would you feel then?* I don't know how I would feel. I hope, though, that I would at some point forgive them, but I don't know if I would.

These are bad people, I remember thinking as I drove away from the old Territorial Prison that night, but they knelt before me and begged God to forgive them and wouldn't leave until I absolved them. We shared a sacred meal together, and I tried to preach to them the Gospel of hope. Maybe they are bad people, but they are also sons and daughters of God.

I was wrong. The Territorial Prison is not a God-forsaken place. No place is. If this isn't evidence of God's mercy, I don't know what is.

Living Memory

You begin to forget little things: Where you left your car keys; the name of an acquaintance you haven't seen in twenty years. Dates and places you could rattle off before now settle on the tip of your tongue, where they languish. Eventually, you forget everything. The stories of your life, all of them, are erased; they slowly evaporate, and with them, go any real sense or notion of identity, of personhood.

Alzheimer's Disease is a thief in the night. Having cased the joint for months, even years, this thief begins to take things from you. First it's the seemingly insignificant tokens that are replaceable. Then, lulling you into a false sense of peace, the thief takes the things that really matter: heirlooms and mementos and trophies, leaving mere dust outlines on the shelf. Then, one day, everything is gone. Everyone you once knew disappears. Whatever grace might be had in this drip, drip, drip of growing amnesia, whatever hope might be harvested, is hidden. You go to God with no memory of God even existing.

❀ ❀ ❀ ❀ ❀ ❀ ❀

Tom Leary and his bride, Betty, have been married for sixty-seven years. They raised eight children: seven of their own and Betty's niece, who came to live with them after her mother died and her father, Betty's brother, could no longer raise her. Their fourth child, Terry, is my oldest brother Brian's wife.

Like many old married couples, Tom and Betty are spiritually conjoined. It's not that they complete each other's sentences or that one naturally assumes to know what the other is thinking or feeling. But seeing them together, you simply cannot tell where one ends and the other begins. This is love. It is tough. It is enduring.

Tom is eighty-nine years old and suffers from Alzheimer's. He and Betty live together in a modest apartment where they still share the same bed. One of their daughters once suggested that they get twin beds so that Betty could sleep comfortably through the night and not be awakened or bruised by Tom's involuntary kicking. "We've slept in the same bed for sixty-seven years," Betty told her. "I'm not going to stop now."

Tom grew up on Curtiss Street in Denver, Colorado. His dad, Cornelius, who went by the name George, worked on airplanes, the old prop ones that you started by turning the propeller. One day one of those propellers severely injured George's arm and shoulder. Doctors told him he would never really be able to use that arm again. It would remain immobile in a locked position against his chest. "The hell with that," George was purported to have said. He spent months lifting buckets of sand until he regained full use of his injured appendage.

Tom's dad went on to invent the kick-starter for motorbikes (which might help explain his granddaughter Terry's near-fetish for all things Harley-Davidson) and the moveable scaffold used for servicing small aircraft.

Like father, like son. There were hints of Tom's indomitable spirit early on. As a young boy, he was leaning too far out of his second-story bedroom window and fell out, landing on the sidewalk below. He bruised a bone and sprained an ankle, but that was it. He walked away relatively unscathed. A natural athlete in high school, Tom was all-city in track and played football. He loves to tell the story of the game when he got hit so hard it knocked him out. Regaining consciousness, he returned to the field and finished the game. At least his coach and teammates told him this. Tom had no memory of the game whatsoever.

Tom's younger brother Ed was equally tough. He was a ball turret gunner in a B-17 Flying Fortress during World War II. Scrunched into position in the ball turret located on the belly of the aircraft, Ed flew on missions over Germany and was shot down once. Tom and Betty's family became "Uncle Ed's" family, since he never married himself. In sixty-seven years, he's never missed a Christmas, an Easter, or a Thanksgiving at the Leary household, except for the war years.

Tom never got a college degree. Attending the local community college in Los Angeles where his family had relocated, Tom spent the rest of his day working for Calavo Growers, an avocado farm in the valley. Tom applied his natural computer know-how and completely streamlined the way the company did payroll, inventory, and billing. Someone from IBM got wind of this and offered Tom a job with IBM. When they opened their first office in San Jose in the early 1950s, they picked Tom to go there and help get things up and running. He was there at the birth of the modern computer age, back when computer hard drives were three-and-a-half-feet tall and two-feet wide and probably held only one megabyte of memory.

Tom met the love of his life while in Los Angeles. They courted and fell in love. Betty converted to Catholicism and they were married. They settled in San Jose and had seven children. Tom became a worker of wood (he once built a second story to a house for a woman and her children when the husband and father suddenly died) and a reader of books and a computer geek. He became a jokester, a prankster, and a lover of the tale.

Much of this Tom probably no longer remembers. These are stories my brother's wife, Terry, and her brothers and sisters remember and hold on to for dear life. Remembering is a supreme act of mercy; it reflects love that is fierce and formidable. What Alzheimer's succeeds in stealing, mercy reclaims and safeguards and protects. As the father loosens his grip and from his weary fingers fall fragile, breakable things, the children are there to catch them lest they fall to the ground and shatter. Not to have someone, anyone, there at such a moment truly is the greatest poverty.

"Can a woman forget her nursing child," Yahweh asks his chosen ones in Isaiah 49, "or show no compassion for the child of her womb? Even these may forget, yet I will never forget you." Sometimes mothers and fathers do forget. But we, their children, remember for them. And in this, we experience the One who always remembers. Even should Alzheimer's erase every footprint, every fingerprint of memory, including any memory of God, God will remember.

❈ ❈ ❈ ❈ ❈ ❈

My sister-in-law Terry spends a lot of time with her mother and father these days. She drives them to doctor's appointments and helps with the shopping. She does the laundry and the cooking. She puts lotion on their feet and arms and legs so they don't become dry and crackly; and she tends to a simple garden courtyard that rests outside her parent's residence. Her brothers and sisters pitch in too. They call most every day, and those who live away visit often. And since they are captive to their Irish lineage, my hunch is that they spend a lot of time telling stories, the older and more tattered the better. But mostly, I think Terry and her brothers and sisters listen…to the Bing Crosby baritone of their father's voice, to his gentle humming, to every word he utters. These things are worth remembering. Much has been entrusted to them now. They are caretakers of the stories of a man who is alive but can no longer tell stories himself. They have become the father's living memory.

Sometimes mothers and fathers do forget. But we, their children, remember for them. And in this, we experience the One who always remembers.

Andre Dubus reflected upon much of this from a wheelchair that held his broken body. "So my crippling is a daily and living sculpture of certain truths"; he wrote, "we receive and we lose, and we must try to achieve gratitude; and with that gratitude to embrace with whole hearts whatever of life that remains after the losses. No one can do this alone, for being absolutely alone finally means a life not only without people or God or both to love, but without love itself."

We the children become—as it should be—the living memory for our parents. It is our way of staring down the darkness and reminding ourselves and each other that love has no rival.

We begin to forget little things. And in the end we may forget everything. But God won't. God will never forget.

A Terrible Beauty

When explorer David Folsom first laid his eyes on what is now Yellowstone National Park in 1869, he was transfixed by the magnificence of its deep canyon, its lush forests, its serene meadows. Overlooking the canyon one day, he took out his notebook and jotted down the words "magnificent, grand, sublime, awful, a terrible beauty." Folsom could very well have been describing the geography of God's mercy.

From the moment God uttered the words, "Let there be light," He found the universe and our blue planet in particular a place He could call home. It should not come as a surprise to us that the mountains testify to his glory still, that the valleys and the plains speak of His goodness. Is it any wonder when we come to a flowing river or lapping sea, or when we wander in the woods or trek through the desert, that we hear the echo of an ancient song of grace and beauty: God's lullaby for a weary world?

It is a canticle of compassion and forgiveness, sung by the divine troubadour. It jogs our stifled memories and speaks to our minds and hearts of a love that has no rival. It makes saints out of sinners and God into our neighbor. Mountain and river, ocean and desert, valley, plain, and forest all sing of the "terrible beauty" of God's mercy; it is as if all of creation is forever conspiring to reunite God with humanity once and for all, by reminding us of who we were at the very start of things and how things were before the great separation. The earth reminds us, in its own inimitable way, that God has never changed His tune. The work of mercy is the greatest expression of God's love for His beloved. And as surely as it echoes throughout the geography of creation, it reverberates in every human heart. For it is there, too, that God has made His home.